101 SMALL RULES for a BIG JOB SEARCH

NEW GUIDELINES FOR TODAY'S JOB SEEKER

TONY BESHARA

A SAVIO REPUBLIC BOOK
An Imprint of Post Hill Press

ISBN: 978-1-68261-368-9
ISBN (eBook): 978-1-68261-369-6

101 Small Rules for a Big Job Search:
New Guidelines for Today's Job Seeker
© 2017 by Anthony Beshara
All Rights Reserved

Cover Design by Quincy Avilio

Published in the United States of America

ACKNOWLEDGMENTS

Greatest thanks go to Chrissy for her prayers, time, and spiritual support. A great deal of thanks goes also to Austin Miller and Nena Madonia and all the folks at Dupree Miller & Associates. A special thanks goes out to Flora Herbert, our Director of Research, who has been so helpful in researching and editing. Thank you also goes to the thousands of candidates and employers who have provided the "real-life" advice contained in these pages.

DEDICATION

This book is dedicated to God, life, and God's greatest blessings: my wonderful wife and best friend, Chrissy, and our wonderful family.

TABLE OF CONTENTS

INTRODUCTION

Looking for a job today is more difficult than it's ever been. I've been helping people find jobs since 1973 (before fax machines... and those were going to "revolutionize" looking for a job). Back then, companies ran ads in the local newspaper to attract good candidates. People mailed their résumés. They telephoned employers—the phones were black with a dial—and got interviews and tried to get the job.

Obviously, things are a lot more complicated today. The internet *has* revolutionized the way we look for a job. The global economy affects us all. The distance between a job candidate and the job itself is farther away than it has ever been, and there are more hurdles and hoops that a job candidate has to jump over and jump through. Finding a job is harder than ever.

There are thousands of books, including mine, articles, online programs, and advisors that provide information about getting a job in today's market. I've interviewed more than 29,000 job candidates and personally found jobs for more than 11,000 of them on a one-on-one basis. I am asked all the time, "Tony, what's the one most important *rule* about_____?" The blank could be filled in with any of these words: preparing for a job search, when I should start my job search, looking for a job when you have one, résumés, sending your résumés, to whom I should send the résumés, who I should call, what I should say, when I should interview, how I should interview, and so forth.

With this in mind, I thought it would be appropriate to write about today's job search "rules." A short, to the point book of job search rules is in order. These are the most important rules of each subject my candidates and I follow to find jobs. Volumes can be written about some of the subjects, for instance, résumés. I offer the most important rules about résumés, but if your résumé is working for you, you may not need the advice. The purpose of this book is to give quick, right to the point rules of a job search. If the reader is following some of the rules, they can simply check them off and move on to others. If they're not following some, they need to get the message and change what they can.

The purpose of this book is to be a short, quick guide to the 101 rules for a successful job search.

PART ONE
RULES FOR PREPARATION

*There are no secrets to success. It is the
result of preparation, hard work, and
learning from failure.*

—Colin Powell

1. PREPARE YOURSELF FOR THE EMOTIONAL STRAIN OF A JOB SEARCH.

The first big "shock" most job seekers confront is the emotional strain of having to look for a job. Next to death of a spouse, death of a child, or death of a parent (coupled with divorce), the fourth most emotionally stressful thing people do is look for a job. That first shock is amplified even more if a person lost a job unexpectedly. Being laid off or fired abruptly, without knowing in any way that it is coming, makes things even more difficult. For some reason, most job candidates don't *expect* an emotional roller coaster. They have a tendency to think that the other guy is going to have emotional ups and downs, but not them.

The first step is to expect emotional strain. Recognize that there are going to be phenomenal emotional peaks and valleys. Expect to go from sad to mad to encouraged to deflated to in control to powerless to courageous to scared to energized to exhausted...all in one day. Then, you will wake up the next day and repeat the cycle. The cycle itself can be exhausting.

There is very little you can do to avoid the emotional strain. In fact, if you don't experience it you're probably not committed enough to finding a job. However, you can *manage* the emotional ups and downs. If most all of the rules laid out are followed, even the rules that don't seem "emotional," a job seeker's confidence will be so strong that the impact of the emotions will be minimal.

2. WORK ON YOUR ATTITUDE. READ AND LISTEN TO MOTIVATIONAL STUFF EVERY DAY.

One of the most difficult challenges in a job search, especially in today's market, is maintaining a positive attitude. Rule #1 is the foundation of a negative attitude. Unfortunately, the majority of things that happen to job seekers are negative. You send 100 résumés and get absolutely no response except rejection emails. You are told by a friend that you'd be perfect for the opening they have in their company and never hear from him. You are told in an initial interview that you are perfect for the job and never get called back. You are told you are going to get a job offer and then you never hear from the company or the hiring authority again. In fact, my estimate is that there are fifteen of these types of negative things that happen for every positive event.

It wouldn't hurt for a job seeker to read the following every day. It was written by one of my first teachers, Jim Rohn:

The process of human change begins within us. We all have tremendous potential. We all desire good results from our efforts. Most of us are willing to work hard and to pay the price that success and happiness demand.

Each of us has the ability to put our unique human potential into action and to acquire a desired result. But the one thing that determines the level of our potential that produces the intensity of our activity, and predicts the quality of the result we receive, is our attitude.

Attitude determines how much of the future we are allowed to see. It decides the size of our dreams and influences our determination when we are faced with new challenges. No other person on earth has dominion over our attitude. People can affect our attitude by teaching us poor thinking habits or unintentionally misinforming us or providing us with negative sources of influence, but no one can control our attitude unless we voluntarily surrender that control.

No one else "makes us angry." We make ourselves angry when we surrender control of our attitude. What others may have done is irrelevant. We choose, not they. They merely put our attitude to a test. If we select a volatile attitude by becoming hostile, angry, jealous, or suspicious, then we have failed the test. If we condemn ourselves by believing that we are unworthy, then again, we have failed the test.

If we care at all about ourselves, then we must accept full responsibility for our own feelings. We must learn to guard against those feelings that have the capacity to lead our attitude down the wrong path and to strengthen those feelings that can lead us confidently into a better future.

If we want to receive the rewards the future holds in trust for us, then we must exercise the most important choice given to us as members of the human race by maintaining total dominion over our attitude. Our attitude is an asset, a treasure of great value, which must be protected accordingly. Beware of the vandals and thieves among us who would injure our positive attitude or seek to steal it away.

Having the right attitude is one of the basics that success requires. The combination of a sound personal philosophy and a positive attitude about ourselves gives us an inner strength and a firm resolve that influences all the other areas of our existence.

I suggest job seekers, or anyone, for that matter, be constantly reading positive, motivational books and listening to positive CDs, podcasts, and TED Talks. Fifteen to thirty minutes of this kind of reading every day as part of your routine makes all the difference in the world.

- *Acres of Diamonds* by Russell Conwell and Robert Shackleton
- *As a Man Thinketh* by James Allen
- *Awaken the Giant Within* by Tony Robbins
- *Beyond Strength: Psychological Profiles of Olympic Athletes* by Steven Ungerleider and Jacqueline M. Golding
- *Blink* by Malcom Gladwell
- *Devotional Classics* by Richard J. Foster and James Bryan Smith
- *Don't Sweat the Small Stuff* by Richard Carlson
- *In Pursuit of Excellence* by Terry Orlick
- *In the Zone: Transcendent Experience in Sports* by Michael Murphy and Rhea A. White
- *The Inner Athlete* by Dan Millman
- *Inward Bound* by Alexander Everett
- *Man's Search for Meaning* by Viktor E. Frankl
- *Psycho-Cybernetics* by Maxwell Maltz
- *The Purpose Driven Life* by Rick Warren
- *Selling the Invisible* by Harry Beckwith

- *The Seven Spiritual Laws of Success* by Deepak Chopra
- *Stumbling on Happiness* by Daniel Gilbert
- *Switch: How to Change Things When Change Is Hard* by Chip Heath and Dan Heath
- *The 7 Habits of Highly Effective People* by Stephen R. Covey
- *The Achievement Zone* by Shane Murphy
- *The Book of Five Rings* by Miyamoto Musashi
- *The E-Myth* by Michael E. Gerber
- *The Gift of Adversity* by Norman E. Rosenthal
- *The Inner Game of Tennis* by W. Timothy Gallwey
- *The Intention Experiment* by Lynne McTaggart
- *The Job Search Solution* by Tony Beshara
- *The Laws of Spirit* by Dan Millman
- *The Magic of Thinking Big* by David J. Schwartz
- *Way of the Peaceful Warrior* by Dan Millman
- *The Power of Positive Thinking* by Norman Vincent Peale
- *The Richest Man in Babylon* by George S. Clason
- *Talent Is Overrated* by Geoff Colvin
- *Outliers* by Malcom Gladwell
- *Drive* by Daniel H. Pink
- *Predictably Irrational* by Dan Ariely
- *Presence* by Amy Cuddy
- *Wooden on Leadership* by John Wooden
- *Willpower* by Roy F. Baumeister and John Tierney
- *Flow* by Mihaly Csikszentmihalyi
- *Great by Choice* by Jim Collins and Morten T. Hansen
- *How We Decide* by Jonah Lehrer
- *Nerve* by Taylor Clark
- *Subliminal* by Leonard Mlodinow
- *PEAK, Secrets from the New Science of Expertise* by Anders Ericsson and Robert Pool
- *Make Your Bed* by Admiral William H. McRaven

Spiritual books, like the *Bible*, the *Koran*, *The Bhagavad-Gita*, *Tao Te Ching*, books of prayer, and so forth, are also excellent.

I would recommend "Horatio Alger"-type stories, like those of Helen Keller and Colonel Sanders, or any inspirational stories that talk about lessons people learn by living and succeeding in a terribly "unfair" world. Stories about people overcoming a fear or insurmountable odds to triumph in the end inspire us all.

Recommended Authors of CDs

Jim Rohn, Norman Vincent Peale, Anthony Robbins, Phil McGraw (Dr. Phil), Dennis Waitley, Brian Tracy, Zig Ziglar, Wayne Dyer, Dan Millman, Steven Covey, Dan Pink, Pema Chodron, Brené Brown, Carol Dweck, Jack Canfield, Ron Clark, and Michael Gerber

TED Talks

If you haven't discovered these already, you should know they are well worth exploring. There are thousands of them and most of them are phenomenally uplifting. They are easy to get hooked on. Just Google "TED Talks." One or two a day of the right kind of talk will keep your spirits up. (Especially: *The Principles of People Who Love Their Job and Their Career.*)

3. MANAGE THE PROCESS. YOU WON'T HAVE TO WORRY ABOUT THE RESULT.

Coach John Wooten, the legendary UCLA basketball coach, famously taught that "If you manage the process, you don't have to worry about the score." Most solid businesses operate with the same principle. The same is true with the job search.

You *can't* control getting a job offer. You *can* control the right steps it takes to get a job.

Just thinking about "getting a job" is way too overwhelming. Thinking about doing all of the steps in the process of getting a job and doing them well is quite manageable. Writing an effective résumé is manageable. Getting that résumé in the right hands of the people may really need your skills is manageable. Calling or emailing potential employers with compelling emails and effective voicemails is manageable. Contacting the hundreds of people you need to contact in order to get an interview is manageable. Designing an effective LinkedIn profile is manageable. An effective initial interview is very manageable. Effective follow-up interviews are manageable. Getting and negotiating a job offer is very manageable.

If you manage the process...you don't have to worry about the result.

4.   PREPARE FOR REALITY. IT'S GOING TO BE A LOT HARDER THAN YOU THINK.

There are millions of out-of-work people in the United States who just plain quit looking for a job. I contend that the majority of the reason this happens is that they are so emotionally stressed out, they resort to doing nothing at all or go through minimal motions in looking for a job. They are scared and often depressed.

There are going to be setbacks after setbacks after setbacks. You are going to have to work harder than you ever imagined just to get an interview. Simply sending a résumé to a job posting isn't going to get you an interview. When you get an interview, you're going to be shocked at the number of people you're going to be competing with. When you think you've interviewed phenomenally well and you're told you will get a call back, you hear absolutely nothing. You wait by the phone expecting the call you were told you were going to get, and it never comes.

The lesson is to be prepared for tons of setbacks and more hard work than you ever imagined. Prepare to be discouraged, disappointed, lied to, dumped on in about every way you can possibly imagine. (I even run into candidates all the time who have been scammed by folks who claim that if you send them $5,000 they will "expose you" to the hidden job market. There is no such thing.) I knew one candidate, not too long ago, who realized that the negatives were going to be 10 or 15 to 1 relative to the positives, so he kept counting the negative events. His rationale was "every negative is one more step towards a positive." Not a bad approach.

5. QUIT WHINING AND GET OVER IT. LIFE ISN'T FAIR.

Interviewing and hiring are staged, contrived events. But, as Churchill said about democracy, it's "the worst form of government, except all those others that have been tried from time to time." The kind of interviewing and hiring process the business world has adopted is the best we've got.

Candidates complain that hiring authorities ask very unfair questions that have nothing to do with the job (i.e., "Why are manholes round?" and "What is one thing about you that you don't want me to know?") and employers get hung up on one or two answers that aren't the way *they* would answer the question (i.e., define "consultative selling"). We have seen candidates and hiring authorities get hung up on the smallest, silliest things that really have nothing to do with a candidate's ability to do the job or the quality of a job opportunity.

There is no sense in getting mad or disappointed about things like this. When they happen, the situations *are* unfair—not right, just *unfair*—but, so is life. Get over it and move on. You'll hardly ever rectify or change the situation. Accept what you may not understand and move on. If you get stuck in the emotional rut of the interviewing and hiring process being unfair, or even try to understand it, it will get in the way of an effective job search. Get over it!

6. PRACTICE CALMING THE SPIRIT.

Having done this since 1973, I guarantee you that there is a spiritual side of looking for a job that is tremendously overlooked. Those of us who believe in a relationship with God are profoundly aware of the spiritual encounter, but even those with more of a secular, humanistic "connection" with "the universe" will benefit from spiritual practice.

Looking for a job is a tremendously emotional endeavor. It is an emotional roller coaster. Enduring it is easier for those who practice spiritual giving. Here are some of the things that I've learned from candidates and employers along the way.

- **Be nice.** Even when other people aren't. You are going to experience a tremendous amount of rejection and frustration. Focus on being nice when they don't feel like it.
- **Create flow.** Clean out your garage, your attic, your car, your office. "Stuff" blocks flow. Put things in order. Remember, external order creates internal calm.

- **Practice forgiveness,** especially when other people are rude and what you perceive to be mean. Forgive those who put you on hold, forget about you, tell you they're going to get back to you and don't, and so on. Send an email to an old nemesis forgiving them.
- **Start an intentions or prayer list.** Pray for those who are less fortunate than you. Be specific about the individuals, even people you don't know. Write their names down. Hopefully, others are doing the same for you.
- **Volunteer.** At soup kitchens, Habitat for Humanity, and so forth. Give time to those less fortunate than you.
- **Be grateful.** Every morning when you wake up and at night before you sleep, acknowledge every blessing you have regardless of every difficulty and challenge.
- **Seek peace.** Spend 10 or 15 minutes twice a day quietly sitting alone getting in touch with your feelings and thoughts. Just let them flow.
- **Pray.** Even if you don't believe in it, prayer works.
- **Meditate.** Not far off from "seeking peace" is meditation. It's the practice of clearing the mind and finding that gap between conscious and subconscious.
- **Let go.** Envision an image of what bad feelings look like. Put them up close to your face in color and then send them far out into the horizon. As they go out further from you, turn their color into black and white, and as they become a small speck, drop them in the ocean. Do this five times with each difficult thought or emotion and you'll be amazed at the relief.

- **Journal.** Simply sit down and write out your thoughts and feelings of the day. A spiral notebook is fine, just date every entry. The entries don't have to be long. One or two sentences might be fine for an uneventful day. A day full of angst or excitement, positive or negative events, may need more than just a couple of sentences. Reviewing these from time to time "objectifies" our emotions.
- **Fast.** This is a great sacrifice and it leads to a tremendous number of other disciplines. It may sound like a big deal, but fasting only one day a week isn't really that hard. Make sure that you are healthy enough to do this and consult your doctor if you think you should try it.

7. DEVELOP RITUALS AND ROUTINES.

I can't tell you how important it is to maintain a daily routine. Even a highly regimented schedule while looking for a job is best. There is so much doubt, uncertainty, and fear involved in looking for a job that a highly regimented schedule gives you the comfort of process. Focus on the process of getting a job rather than just the result. Focusing on the result of getting a job, by itself, is too difficult to do, but focusing on the process of getting a job—doing all the things you need to do to get a job—is much more controllable.

I recommend that, if you're out of work and able to look for a job full-time, which sometimes gives you a lot more focus than having to look for a job while you're keeping one, develops a strict daily routine that you can religiously follow. For instance, wake up every morning at exactly the same time, dress in business attire just as though you were going to a job, and lay out a structured day.

A highly regimented schedule saves time for thinking and allows the job seeker to focus energy on the most important aspect of the job search, getting and performing well on interviews. Set aside the first two or three hours of the morning, when you don't have interviews, to cold calling and sending résumés, as well as following up those résumés with phone calls and e-mails. Try to schedule interviews at about the same time every day.

There are numerous standard computer programs that provide a great daily calendar, and they are very easy to use. A calendar creates a situation where you don't have to rely on your memory. Worrying about the things you need to remember uses a tremendous amount of emotional and physical energy.

Over the past number of years, various researchers have shown that making conscious decisions—any kind of conscious decision, from "Which shirt should I wear?" to "What should I eat?"—tires your brain, like getting muscle fatigue from exercise. Following a daily routine keeps you from having to make conscious decisions about trivial things that tire out your brain and deplete energy you need for the most important things, such as getting and doing well on interviews. Even having the same thing for breakfast every morning helps.

Develop a very strict routine and save your emotional and mental energy for the most important things in your job search.

8. SET GOALS, DAILY AND WEEKLY.

Looking for a job is hard enough, but if you don't set daily and weekly goals, it's going to get much harder. Looking for a job, even if you have one, is such a multifaceted beast that people have to set daily and weekly goals. I emphasize *process*, as you will learn, and part of the job search process is to be meaningful and will center around goals.

Setting goals is really simple and most people want to overlook it in order to get to "what matters," like interviewing and getting a job. The daily and weekly goals, recited daily as affirmations, become part of the systematic approach to getting a job.

In short, goals need to be: *S.M.A.R.T.* It's a very old adage that works. Goals need to be Specific, Measurable, Attainable, Realistic, and Trackable. They need to be stated in the personal present tense, with as much sensory language as possible. There are 14 million articles about goals if one Googles "how to set goals." You certainly don't need to read 14 million, but a few of the very first ones will suffice to get the hang of it. A sample goal in your job search, if you are looking for a job full-time, would be something like this:

> *"It is Monday of the second week of my job search. I see myself making twenty 'cold calls' this morning to connect directly with people I know. I hear myself leaving an excellent, well-scripted presentation of myself to prospective employers. I hear the phone ring as at least 10% of them call me back inquiring about my experience. I feel the wonderful feeling and excitement about them making a face-to-face appointment with me."*

I'm quite certain you get the hang of it. There should be no more than ten goals like this and they should be just as specific.

9. RECITE AFFIRMATIONS DAILY.

As people set goals, they need to turn those goals into affirmations. This is a matter of taking four or five of these goals and turning them into affirmations that one recites every day, "embedding" those instructions into the subconscious.

This is really simple to do. It's simply a matter reciting your goals out loud every day (after you pray and meditate). So you cannot only hear them, but even *feel* them.

10. LOSE WEIGHT AND GET FIT.

This is one of the most difficult and challenging rules to deal with. It gets personal with lots of people, and they often get not only uncomfortable, but are insulted by this rule. Honestly, it is often very difficult to implement.

It is so easy when a person is going through an emotionally stressful experience, like looking for a job, to begin to neglect lots of personal disciplines. It's very common for job seekers to express their emotional strain by overeating and gaining weight. It could happen so fast, one bite at a time, especially comfort foods that add weight. And then, what's even worse, their clothes begin to look tight because they've gained weight. It is really easy to scoff about this idea, but it happens so very often that we needed to make a rule about it.

It is even a better idea to get physically fit. In days of uncertainty and fear, especially if you are out of work, the discipline of exercise and getting into shape is one of the best things you can do. Consistent, daily, or at least three times a week exercise programs are another great way to develop rituals that carry over into interviewing to getting hired.

11. THE JOB MARKET IS GETTING BETTER (ONLY IF YOU THINK SO).

It's a great time to find a job:

- Low unemployment (4.4%)
- Companies have money on the side
- Corporate profits are up
- Workers are returning to the workforce faster than anticipated
- 24% of employers in the U.S. plan to increase staff in the next year (Manpower Employment Outlook Survey—Q3 2016)
- Opportunity to brush up on soft skills, such as decision-making, self-motivation, leadership skills and teamwork skills, tap into your network, focus more on your job search
- Wages rose 4.7% over the last year, whereas the increase from 2009 through the end of 2013 averaged only 3.1%. That falls short of the 6.1% average gain from 1980 through 2007, but it still represents a significant improvement (Bureau of Economic Analysis)

12. THE JOB MARKET IS GETTING WORSE (ONLY IF YOU THINK SO).

It's a lousy time to find a job:

- 62.9% labor participation rate (lowest level since 1977)
- Compliance issues cause companies to lose focus on hiring

15

- There are so many compliance laws that businesses are constricting
- Corporate taxes at 35% and companies moving overseas along with the jobs
- Wages are falling because there's lots of competition
- Middle class is losing ground and getting hallowed out
- America is going part-time, and not because it's fun
- Union wages are harder to come by
- Inequality is getting worse, in that salary gaps between men and women are increasing
- Entrepreneurship has declined in the past six years
- Ballooning student loan debt

13. PEOPLE ARE A PAIN IN THE ASS AND THEY'RE ANNOYING. THEY DON'T CARE ABOUT YOU. THEY ARE SPIRITUAL BEINGS ACTING HUMAN.

It was Pierre Teilhard de Chardin, the Jesuit philosopher, who wrote, "We are not human beings having a spiritual experience. We are spiritual beings having a human experience." In the everyday world, our human experience and being human seems to grossly overshadow our desire to reach the higher level of spirituality. In fact, people are a pain in the ass. And so are you!

Unfortunately, most people in a job search are going to painfully "experience" the human side of lots of people—the pain in the ass side. And that human side ranges anywhere from insensitive to downright rude. These are the people, hiring authorities, interviewing authorities, even friends of yours, anyone you encounter in the job search, who don't return your calls, leaving you hanging with the statement, "We'll get back to you" and never do. Or they tell you what they think at the moment that turns out to not be the truth (lie!), like, "You're perfect for this job..." and then after the interview, perpetual silence.

You know that you are vulnerable; looking for a job is very emotional and difficult. You are sensitive to what people tell you and how they treat you and often, it just isn't nice. It's very hard to deal with and almost impossible to understand from your point of view. You are sensitive, oftentimes downright afraid. You take it all personally.

By recognizing that these people are spiritual beings acting human, it will be easier for you to be kind, patient, understanding and even forgiving. Your anger and frustration is understandable. Realize that these people are often bumbling through their lives the way many others, including you, are. They really only care about themselves and running a successful business. They only care about you to the extent that you can help them run their business and be successful.

By recognizing that they are "acting human" you will feel better. It might make you more sensitive to the times that you are more human than spiritual.

14. TAKE MASSIVE ACTION. HOPE IS NOT A STRATEGY. ACTION CONQUERS FEAR.

I'm continually amazed how lackadaisical and reactive job-search candidates are. For most folks about the most proactive thing they do in a job search is call a few of their friends, acquaintances, a recruiter or two and then, the ultimate job-search activity—send résumés over the internet. They send and hope, send and hope, hope and send, and send and hope. Hope is not a strategy! And then they tell me that they're looking for a job really hard.

The most successful job seekers are the ones who are very, very proactive. They don't just "send" a résumé to a company. They pick up the phone and call the manager of the department that they would be applying to, present themselves as a job candidate, and actually ask for a face-to-face interview. They don't sit and wait for the phone to ring. They pick up the phone and they call at least 35 to 40 people a day—people they know and people they don't know—and make a presentation on themselves to a hiring authority while asking for a face-to-face interview. They leave voicemails with a great presentation about themselves and encourage the potential hiring authority to call them.

These people will find LinkedIn connections to people and organizations they would like to interview with. They call these connections and ask for support to get an interview. They will actually sit in the lobby of a hiring authority's office unannounced and try to get an appointment with him or her. They do whatever they can to make as many contacts and get as many interviews as possible. And they don't stop even when they get rejected and refused.

They realize that getting refused and rejected is simply a "no." They know that they will have to get 15 to 20 "no" answers before they get a "yes." It's nothing personal; it simply means that someone else is going to get the opportunity to hire them. I know some of these candidates who actually count the "no" responses and celebrate them knowing that they are one more "no" toward a "yes."

These kinds of candidates push to get themselves interviews. Once they do, they prepare themselves extremely well for the interview. They practice the presentation of themselves so they have it down to as close to perfection as they can get. They are aware of their strengths and weaknesses in the eyes of the hiring authority. They sell themselves to their strengths and are aware of their own vulnerabilities. They sell their features, advantages, and benefits. They end each interview by asking the interviewing authority their opinion about how they stack up with the other candidates being interviewed, if the hiring authority has any concerns about their ability to do the job, and then they ask the most important question, "What do I need to do to get the job?"

These people are relentless in getting as many interviews as they can even though they think they might be getting offers. They proactively follow up every interview with not only a thank you but a summary of the interview and a phone call to the hiring or interviewing authority thanking them for their time and asking for a follow-up interview.

These kinds of candidates never stop focusing on the process, the proactive process of getting initial interviews, performing well on the initial interviews, getting follow-up interviews, performing well on all follow-up interviews, making themselves unique in the eyes of the interviewing or hiring authority, and then asking for a job. They are always in control of numerous interview cycles. They follow this process over and over and over until they find a job they really like.

15. DON'T QUIT YOUR JOB!

This is a rule that many people have to learn the hard way and then, it's way too late. I can't tell you the number of people over the years who just plain got fed up with what they were doing and, worse, thought anyone in their right mind would hire them. They thought that a new job would be easy to find so they quit their job. They find out five or six months later that quitting a job before they had another one was a really big mistake.

Lots of people have a tendency to "read their own press clippings." They have a tendency to think that because they've had such a meteoric rise where they are, or that they're doing so well at their own firm, every company out there in their right mind would want to hire them. They really have no idea what the job market is like and since they are often listening to their spouses, friends, relatives, and so forth, who are telling them that the "sun rises and sets" with them, they quit their job. Unless they get incredibly lucky, it is something they'll wish they had never done.

So, unless your current job gets totally untenable, such as if you can never interview because you travel 100% of the time, don't quit your job unless you have a new one.

16. START NOW.

Don't put off starting a job search. Often, when people are let go from their job, the first thing they do is to "take time off" to relax and unwind. The longer they do this, the harder it is to start a job search. In fact, people who begin their job search right away after they get laid off find a job, on average, six weeks faster than those people who do not. It is simply just too easy to relax, take a trip, visit family, and get into a groove of doing nothing towards looking for a job. The longer it goes, the more likely it is to continue; weeks become months and pretty soon the candidate is having to explain what he or she has been doing the last six months. Saying to a prospective employer something like, "Well, I took the last six months off to decompress after my job ended," is a kiss of death. The employer thinks, "Well, if this person can afford to take six months off without a job, they must not need a job very badly and if I hire them, they might be here six weeks and just decide to take more time off...pass!"

If people need a little time to "clear their head," the best way is to start planning a job search immediately when they need to. It's better to find a job and then take a short vacation before the job starts. But, if it's absolutely necessary to spend a little time relaxing, initiate a job search plan and take three or four "first steps," and then take a few days off (never more than three or four) and get back to the job search.

As I mention often, the momentum of taking "massive action" with a high sense of urgency propels the most successful job searches.

17. GET "GRIT."

Psychologists, in recent years, have studied the relationship between persistence and creative achievement and have cited that most creative people have a phenomenal ability to stick with their work in spite of all the difficulties and challenges they face. The technical term used for this trait is *grit*.

It made me realize that one of the reasons we have so many people in America who actually just give up looking for a job when they need one is that they lack grit.

Many of these people who give up looking for a job just plain don't know what to do. After talking to a few friends and family they resort to hitting the send button with their résumé attached, thinking that is the work of "looking for a job." Grit in looking for a job has to do with developing a job search strategy and executing on that strategy no matter how hard or difficult it may be. It is putting up with the ups and downs of the job search: the rejection, the refusal, the not getting called back, being told you're the "best candidate" and then never hearing from the folks who told you that. Grit is what it takes to keep on keeping on, in spite of setbacks.

Grit is focusing on the process and not worrying about the results, even when it's emotionally difficult. It is making one more call after 15 or 16 rejections in a row. It's overcoming the downright depressive, rejected feeling when you don't get hired to give you the moxie to immediately go to another interview.

Get grit by:

- Encouraging a growth mind-set. Individuals with a growth mind-set believe intelligence and talent can be developed through hard work and dedication. By contrast, those with a fixed mind-set believe a person's most basic abilities are fixed traits.
- Perseverance (perseverance is the pursuit; grit is the trait).
- Hard work. Like pushing yourself to make 10 more cold calls about yourself, *right after* you have been rejected.
- Drive to improve. Get better at what you do daily. Get more interviews. Interview better. Follow up on those interviews better. Drive to improve.
- Self-regulating. Don't let others take your "power" away from you.
- Pushing yourself. If you don't end the day feeling mentally and emotionally depleted, you probably haven't worked very hard.
- Focusing. Focus on what you can control and mentally and emotionally let go of the things you can't control.

18. FIX YOUR EMAILS TO GET ATTENTION.

Make sure that your emails are short and to the point. Keep this in mind when you write an email. There are 205 billion emails sent and received every day in the world. Business people average 126 emails sent and received daily, according to the The Radicati Group, Inc., a worldwide technology research firm based in Palo Alto, California. Hiring authorities and human resources departments receive one and one half times the average. So, picture someone who's looking at 189 emails every day. You tell me if you think your four-paragraph email accompanied by your résumé is going to be read. It's not!

Your email, preferably introducing yourself and your résumé, should be short. I recommend no longer than two or three paragraphs with no longer than two or three sentences. Remember that the email, like your résumé, is going to be *scanned*, not read.

The purpose of your email is to get someone to interview you! (At the least, read your résumé.)

An effective "subject" line might be "Excellent salesperson," "Outstanding accountant," "Efficient administrator," and so on, followed by maybe one or two sentences, highlighted with:

- Reached 120% of quota three years in a row
- Lowered department expenses 15% three years in a row
- Increased efficiency 20%
- Lowered turnover 15%

Put these in the body of the email. Remember that "stories sell...numbers tell." Then write a short, succinct email selling yourself with numbers that say "I'm a good employee, and you should interview me."

A three- or four-paragraph email is *not* going to get read! This also applies to LinkedIn InMails.

One last thought about your emails. Make sure you put your telephone number under your name or your "signature." That way it's easy for people to call you.

19. FIX YOUR VOICEMAILS TO GET ATTENTION.

Make sure you confirm the number of your cell phone *and* your name with your recorded voicemail message. You want to be sure that people know exactly who they are reaching. Be sure to record your voicemail message in a quiet place, not while driving, not while in a Starbucks. Not only is it unprofessional, but the caller may not call back if they can't understand exactly who they've reached. (By the way, many of us keep résumés for specific types of people for many years. From my own experience, if I call a phone number that is more than two or three years old and I'm not sure the phone number is of the person I'm trying to reach—i.e., they don't state their name in the voicemail message—I might not leave a message. I'll simply hang up.)

PART TWO
RULES FOR GETTING AN INTERVIEW

*The journey of 1,000 miles begins with
one step.*

– Lao Tzu

---

20. NEXT TO GETTING A JOB OFFER, GETTING AN INTERVIEW AND PERFORMING WELL ON AN INTERVIEW ARE THE MOST IMPORTANT THINGS YOU CAN DO.

There is so much "noise" out there about how to get a job and so many people saying so many things, it's hard to separate the right stuff from the junk. I recently saw a video by a "job search expert" who talked about how important it was for candidates to have a blog and all of the effort it takes to write a blog, and so on.

Please remember that the most important thing you can do to get a job is to interview well. The second most important thing you can do to get a job is to get the interview. You gotta pick up the phone, call a hiring authority who has "pain," i.e., the need to hire somebody, and ask for an interview. Then go to the interview and sell yourself.

I interview candidates all the time who spend hours upon hours crafting résumés, developing their personal "brand," designing their LinkedIn profile, developing "guerrilla tactics" for their job search, attending seminars, and all kinds of other stuff that cause them to confuse activity with productivity, *instead* of trying to get an interview.

25

The major reason that people spend so much time on all of these secondary activities in looking for a job is because they can control them and they don't run the risk of being rejected by doing them. The sooner a job seeker learns that being rejected is part of a successful job search process, the better off they're going to be.

So, have a nice LinkedIn profile, write a great blog, craft a great résumé, but quit doing this stuff instead of trying to get interviews. Focus on what really matters.

21. EVERYONE KNOWS 200 PEOPLE; 60% OF JOBS ARE FOUND THROUGH PERSONAL CONTACTS.

It's so interesting that people often, when they first go to look for a job, start with perusing websites, sending résumés to online advertising and all kinds of relatively "remote" job search activities. The truth is that 60% of jobs are found through some aspect of personal contacts with people; even people who know people you know can help you find a job. So, the very first thing you should do when you need a job, even if you have one, is to reach out to every personal contact you can think of. These are people like relatives (even distant ones), friends (even long-lost ones), people you worked with in the past, people you've worked with recently, people you graduated from high school with, people you graduated from college with, people in your town who are alumni of your college (you can find them on LinkedIn), people at your church, people at your kids' schools, obviously your neighbors... anyone you can think of.

Joe Girard, the famous car salesperson who wrote a book on sales, says that everyone knows at least 200 people. And those people know 200 people. The thing to start out doing when you need a job is to systematically call everyone you know and ask them about people that they know so that you can call them. Now, I know that this takes a lot of courage and some people will say, "Well, I really don't want to impose on other people like that." Well, let me ask you, which is more uncomfortable: needing a job or not having a job and calling these people? The answer is obvious. Besides, you wouldn't mind it if people called you if the shoe was on the other foot.

So, make a list of everybody you know. Call those people, explain to them that you are looking for a job and you'd like to know if they might know of anybody who could use your kind of skills. If they say "no," which the vast majority of them will, ask them for a referral (I know it takes courage) and then— this is very important—ask them if you can call them back in 45 days to see if they might have thought of anybody who might need your skills. Ninety-nine percent of them will say that it's okay to do that. Then systematically call these people every 45 days. You will be absolutely shocked at the third or fourth time when one of these people will say something like, "Oh, yeah, you know, my boss asked me if I knew of anybody like you about six weeks ago. I can't believe I didn't think of you! Yeah! Give me your résumé and I'll give it to my boss." And you sit there thinking, "You schmuck! I called you 45 days ago, you told me you didn't know of anybody who might need my skills. And now you're just remembering somebody!"

Don't get upset, it won't do you any good. Just realize that that's the way people are.

22. SOCIAL MEDIA IS YOUR FRIEND.

Since 99.99% of your "social media" presence relating to your job search will be through LinkedIn, we need to have this discussion. As a job seeker, LinkedIn is going to be one of your most important tools. We could write whole books about how to use it in a job search, but following is a summary of the mistakes that people make using LinkedIn looking for a job. Paying attention to these is the best way to make social media your friend in your job search.

THE TOP 10 MISTAKES JOB SEEKERS MAKE USING LINKEDIN

LinkedIn has certainly changed the complexion of looking for a job. Some people will claim it has helped individuals' job searches and some people will claim that it does nothing but make their job search more difficult. Some people claim, for instance, that they won't put their picture on LinkedIn because it reveals their age. Some employers will not consider interviewing a candidate who doesn't have their picture on LinkedIn. The tool, however, is here to stay and we all better make it "our friend." Here are the top 10 mistakes that job seekers make using LinkedIn:

1. Waiting to start using LinkedIn until you are unemployed. You should be a proficient user of LinkedIn before you ever start looking for a job. The best time to start using it is before you need a job in order to expand your professional network among recruiters and hiring managers. It takes time to build a good profile, develop solid relationships and, most importantly, create a profile brand. Getting people to know who you are before you need a job is really important.

2. Not being an "active LinkedIn user." It's not only important to create a well-branded, search-optimized

profile, it's important to know how to be a real user. Get to know all of the features that LinkedIn can provide you before you need them. For instance, the ability to find all of the alumni of your college or university in the area where you live is a great way to seek interviews. You should know how to do this before you start looking for a job.

3. No picture at all, or a bad, inappropriate picture. It may not come as a shock, but a lot of employers won't even consider a candidate who doesn't have his or her picture posted on a LinkedIn profile. And what's just as poor is a bad or inappropriate picture. A picture taken with an old iPhone, in poor light that makes your head look like an egg, does not help you. A picture of you fishing, playing golf, coaching your child's baseball team, or a picture of you with the bear you just shot all communicate someone who is not serious about business. Lots of people think that people who shoot bears are miserable and cruel people and don't want them around their company no matter how good they are. These kinds of pictures end your potential candidacy before it has even begun. The message here is to not give a potential employer a reason to make judgments about you that are not in line with the type of employee profile you want to project.

4. Inaccurate information (seemingly). I can't tell you the number of times I've seen situations where a person's LinkedIn profile did not agree with their résumé— differences in dates of employment, job titles and/ or description, jobs shown one place but not both,

education differences, and so forth. End of discussion and end of consideration.

5. Not having a robust profile. Minimal descriptions of who you worked for and what you've done before not only fails to communicate being proud of what you've done before, but brevity doesn't give people the information that they need to evaluate you. Talk about your previous jobs in very positive terms, preferably with some kind of performance measurements. People like numbers.

6. Not having any, or very few, recommendations or endorsements. You should have at least two recommendations for each job listed in the experience section of your profile and at least 50 skills listed in your "skills" section of your profile so people can find you using those terms.

7. Not having enough contacts. Your goal is to have at least 501 connections on LinkedIn so you have the added branding power of "500+." We've experienced candidates being eliminated, especially for sales opportunities, because they didn't have a significant number of contacts. ("How could a successful salesperson have only 100 contacts?") But even if you're not in sales, you need to have a significant number of contacts. A small number of contacts communicates poor social skills. Remember that business is a "contact sport" and the more contacts you have the better "athlete" you appear to be.

8. Not having a customized LinkedIn URL. This should be used for all your marketing information so people

can reach you quickly. Remember, your first and last name is the #1 searchable term on LinkedIn. So, you want to change your vanity URL to remove all of those unnecessary characters and just have your first and last name, if possible. This will not only provide a nice-looking, branded, LinkedIn URL, but it will also allow you to be found more often for your #1 searchable term on LinkedIn...your first and last names. Also, be sure to include your phone number on your profile where people can easily see it—in the Background Summary section is perfect, or under Advice for Contacting. Keep in mind LinkedIn frowns on putting your phone number in your headline or by your name.

9. The first 35 to 40 characters of your headline are not descriptive. The first 35 or 40 characters need to describe exactly who you are and what you do at a glance. However, simply listing a job title and a company name as your headline is not a brand. It's much better to use every one of the 120 available characters to list those searchable terms that not only tell people what you've done but what you can do for them. People are going to "scan" your profile more than they are going to read it. Your headline needs to capture their interest.

10. Not listing your jobs and companies you worked for in reverse chronological order. People are not interested in the first job you had. They are interested in knowing what you're doing now and then work backwards looking at what you've done before. You should do this just like a résumé.

Quit thinking that a LinkedIn profile really doesn't matter in your job search. It does matter, a lot. In October of 2016 LinkedIn surpassed 414 million users. Every second, two new users sign up for LinkedIn. If you have a poor or dismissive attitude towards LinkedIn, it doesn't matter, but the people who are trying to hire you have a high regard for it. I can't tell you the number of candidates who I've represented whose LinkedIn profile was terrible and my client simply told me that with a LinkedIn profile that poor, they just didn't want to interview them. My candidates inevitably say, "Well, I don't use LinkedIn and it doesn't matter." It does matter! A poor LinkedIn profile communicates to a prospective employer that the candidate couldn't be serious about finding a job.

Other mistakes include:

- Not including the right keywords that best describe what you do.
- Not including your contact information in your Contact Info section.
- Not listing any websites in your Contact Info section.
- Not writing your summary section in "first-person."
- No current company logo displayed on the profile.

Regarding LinkedIn changes, there are two experts I would highly recommend. The first is Wayne Breitbarth, author of *The Power Formula for LinkedIn Success*. He can be found at www. powerformula.net. The other is a good friend of mine, Terry Sullivan, president of Buzzpro, and you can find him at www. linkedin.com/in/terrysullivanmba and www.buzzpro.com. Both help companies and individuals with their LinkedIn profiles. They do charge a fee, but they are well worth it.

These two guys appear on my radio program a couple times a month to discuss LinkedIn. Now that Microsoft owns LinkedIn, lots of things about it are changing more rapidly. Some features of LinkedIn have been expanded, contracted, changed, and dropped. It takes more vigilance than it used to, though for the most part LinkedIn is better. However, you need to keep up with it.

23. SOCIAL MEDIA IS YOUR ENEMY.

There are always unintended consequences that come with any new technology and the negative consequences of social media couldn't be more pronounced than in the disastrous effects it has had on people's job searches. In the last six months, just in our organization, we have had candidates who looked like they were getting job offers *lose* those job offers because of what the prospective employer found on social media. Now keep in mind these are mostly professional, degreed candidates with extensive experience, many of whom were earning well over six figures.

The VP of HR with 20 years of experience who has a link on his signature that takes the reader to his blog. He is a "conspiracy theorist" and blatantly writes about his theories about present and past government officials, i.e., presidents of the United States, secretaries of state, and so on. He didn't get hired.

The sales manager with 15 years of a great track record who has a signature, that, again, sent the reader to a blog claiming that unless you follow Jesus Christ you are going to burn in hell. He got eliminated.

The candidates who were eliminated when their names were Googled who had: mugshots, numerous lawsuits, written a review of a prostitute (of course the candidate claimed it wasn't him), an article implicating them in a case of fraud (even though there were no legal charges), at least three cases of "mistaken identity," i.e., different people with the same name as the candidate who had very, very questionable Google reports.

The candidate whose LinkedIn profile highlighted the candidate as a musician instead of a business professional, or the one whose LinkedIn profile highlighted the candidate's numerous nonprofit volunteer positions, causing the hiring authority to believe the candidate wouldn't focus on the work.

The candidates who were eliminated because of what they had on Facebook: pictures of their recent tattoos, celebrations taking place in bars, profanity, provocative pictures, reports on heavy metal band concerts, inappropriate jokes, race-related comments, political comments, religious comments, alcohol/ drug references, a post on a candidate's wall: "Those of you who are ****(sexually graphic)*** my husband, I know who you are." (Please don't tell me, "Well, all you have to do is set your Facebook page to 'private.'" Even the most elementary hacker knows how to work around that.)

The candidate who texted, "grt interview, I prob got the job, but the guy was a jrk" to one of his friends and it got back to the company and the interviewing authority.

Well, I could go on and on, but you get the picture. Please remember that the kind of candidates we place are usually degreed, highly experienced, and highly successful. The average salary we deal with is $100,000 or more. These people getting eliminated aren't young, punk, uneducated millennials who are looking for hourly work. They are, on the surface, very professional, and still come up with these ridiculous online issues.

We are now beginning to ask *every* candidate, no matter how professional they appear, if they have done thorough research of their own on any and all social media that might contain their name or their likeness. There is now a cottage industry growing up around cleaning up an individual's social media as well as researching all social media for companies considering candidates. Remember, there are more than 500 social media sites...and we stopped counting at 65.

The attitude, especially from millennials, but even older candidates, is paradoxical. On the one hand, they use social media extensively; 88% of millennials get news from Facebook and they use an average of 3.7 social media networks daily. But when it comes to information about them, they claim that social media should not have anything to do with their professional lives. They claim their social life and professional life should be separated and that potential employers should not judge hiring them or not based on what they find on social media. They often get downright pissed off when they get eliminated because of what social media reveals about them.

Fifty percent of employers recently surveyed said that they elected not to hire a seemingly well-qualified candidate because of what they found on social media. A quick Google search will find a CareerBuilder report of a litany of stupid things that people either post or text about their job, an interview, or a company they are looking to work for.

This epidemic is probably going to get worse before it gets better. The lesson is simple: Social media can stand in the way of getting a good job.

24. YOU DON'T HAVE ANYTHING UNTIL YOU HAVE AN OFFER.

A while ago, I got a candidate an interview at a particular company. When I went to tell him about the interview he said, "Oh, I know them."

I convinced him to go on the interview. He got the offer two days later and started at the company on the next Monday.

When I was much younger and much less experienced in this profession, I believed candidates when they said something like this. I figured they ought to know, especially when it is a competitor. Well, they don't. My candidate had no idea what he was talking about. He "checked" the company out with friends of friends of friends of friends who didn't know what they were talking about.

Companies change more rapidly than ever. Going by what someone else says or thinks isn't smart.

Make your own judgment about a job and a company. Interview anywhere you can, with anyone reasonable. You have nothing until you have an offer.

If you don't like the opportunity or the company after you interview, for whatever reason, you can drop out of contention.

And as long as we are at it, interview as well as you can, even if you don't think you will want the job or the company. Sell yourself as hard as possible. You need a job or need to change jobs. Don't let your preconceptions get in your way. You really don't know as much as you think you do. Get in the habit of getting offers.

25. IF YOU ARE EMPLOYED, KEEP YOUR JOB SEARCH CONFIDENTIAL.

At least two or three times a month in our organization (we have more than 20 recruiters) one of our candidates gets fired because their superiors found out that they were looking for a job. They call us, probably because nobody else will listen, and complain that they can't believe they got fired and they have absolutely no idea how their superiors found out. They act like they are absolutely clueless as to how their superiors discovered their job search.

Our average recruiter has been in the recruiting business 16 ½ years. Even I, years ago, was mystified as to how this unfortunate-seeming "miracle" could take place that a candidate could lose his or her job because management found out they were looking. Who would be so unlucky? Candidates would absolutely swear that they had not breathed one sentence to anyone they worked with about looking for a job. Years ago, I began to get an inkling that something was wrong with this picture. There had to be more going on when people are looking for a job confidentially and then got fired because they were found out. One day, as one of my candidates was bemoaning the fact that he just got fired, claiming that he couldn't understand how he got found out, I questioned him a little further. After making the candidate think about who they might have told in their company that they were looking for a job, there was a long, long, long pause. And then they said something in a very slow, whisper: "Well...I can trust Angie...she would never... tell...anyone...here...that...I...might...be...looking...for...a... job" as his voice trails off with the last word. Then he says, in an angry way, "There is just no way Angie would tell anybody that I was looking for a job, just no way...just no way...I swore her to secrecy...I told her in confidence." Ever since then, when this kind of thing happens, I force a candidate to think really hard about who they might have told and inevitably their voice goes from doubt to disbelief. They almost think that the reality will be changed if they state it emphatically enough. As reality sets in, they get madder and madder. How could a friend of theirs do this to them?

Bluntly, all of us have "friends" at work, but they are not the lifelong, do-anything-for-you kind of friends. They are your competitors, even if there is a different department, miles away. Don't even imagine that any of your "work friends" are your close, real friends; they're not and they never will be. They are, at best, acquaintances. And you shouldn't tell acquaintances that you are confidentially looking for a job.

The lesson is, just don't ever, ever, *ever* discuss that you are looking for a job with anyone you work with. I guarantee you it will get out and if you get fired, you'll have no one to blame but yourself.

By the way, every once in a while someone asks me if it's legal for a company to fire you for looking for a job. Yes, it is, 99.99% of the time. In nearly every state, it is perfectly legal for your company to fire you if you're looking for a job.

26. HAVE NO EXPECTATIONS ABOUT OUTCOMES. THE PRAYER OF ST. IGNATIUS OF ANTIOCH.

One of the most discouraging aspects of a job search is for job seekers to continually get disappointed about the unsuccessful outcomes of their activities. When they don't get an interview, they get frustrated. When they do get an interview, but don't do well on it and get rejected, they get frustrated. When they are told that they are a great candidate or when they come in "second" and aren't chosen, they can get downright mad. In fact, this may be one of the biggest reasons people stopped looking for work. They are so frustrated at the outcomes that didn't live up to their expectations, they quit.

We should look to the example of elite athletes to find that they have no expectations for outcomes. They do, and I repeat, do have expectations for their own performance, but they do not have expectations for the outcomes. A batter doesn't go to the plate thinking about winning the game. An elite basketball player doesn't shoot the ball worried about winning the game. They focus on their own expectation of themselves doing their best and letting the score, the result, take care of itself.

Job seekers would have a lot less emotional strain if they had no expectations about outcomes. They should have expectations of their own ability to get a lot of interviews. They should have expectations about their ability to perform really well in initial interviews, but no expectations about moving beyond the initial interview. They should have high expectations of themselves to perform well on secondary interviews, but no expectations about why they did or didn't go beyond the secondary interviews. They should have high expectations of themselves being able to negotiate a job offer, but no expectations about getting the job offer. If job seekers have expectations about outcomes, they will spend most of their time being emotionally flattened.

Maximizing expectations of ourselves and minimizing the expectations of the results allows us to channel our emotions toward what we can control and not lose energy over what we can't control.

St. Ignatius of Antioch coined the phrase "holy indifference." Its meaning was to detach oneself from results, to remain indifferent to being rejected, refused, ignored, forgotten, and lied to. Pray for Holy indifference.

27. KNOW THE ODDS OF GETTING A JOB BY APPLYING TO AN ONLINE POSTING.

There are a number of studies and articles that discuss the success of finding a job by responding to online job postings. Based on what those authors state and *my own experience as a recruiter since 1973*:

- On average, 1,000 to 1,500 individuals view a job posting.
- Between 200 and 275 of these people will begin the application process or send a résumé.
- Between 150 and 180 people will complete an application or send a résumé.
- 90 to 110 of those résumés or applications will be scanned by an ATS or some type of human screener who may or may not know what they are looking for.
- 20 to 25 résumés will be sent to a hiring authority. (Once this number is reached, whoever is reviewing the résumés or applications will stop reviewing them. This means that if you're not in that group, you are likely to be "deleted.")
- 4 to 6 candidates will be invited to interview.
- 1 to 2 of them will be invited back for subsequent and final interviews.
- 25 percent of the time the "search" will start all over because the hiring authority doesn't feel he or she has seen enough quality candidates, or doesn't like what he or she has seen.
- Of the remaining 75 percent of the time, one of the finalists will be offered the job and accept.
- 20 percent of the time, the first candidate offered the job turns it down, then the second candidate is offered the position. If that candidate does not accept the job, which happens about 20 percent of the time, the search starts all over again.

So, based on this reality, what are a candidate's odds of getting hired by submitting a résumé to an online job posting?

Very, very, very slim—about 1 in 375 to 400. No wonder people get discouraged and give up.

28. KEEP YOUR RÉSUMÉ SIMPLE AND TO THE POINT.

The purpose of your résumé is to get you an interview. You want people to look at your résumé and think, "I really must interview this person!" Remember that your résumé does *not* get read, it gets *scanned*. People think, "Oh, my résumé gets read!" No, it doesn't. It gets scanned and the people who scanned them are looking for a few key things: how long you have worked at the companies you've worked for, i.e., exact dates, what you did for them, in very clear terms, and how well you performed. It's that simple.

You have to remember that these people are reviewing 180 to 200 résumés a day. They don't read any of them. They scan them to look for some of the things they are looking for. So, this means that you have to, when you write the name of your company on the résumé, explain what that company does. There are 7.1 million businesses in the United States and I guarantee you the people looking at your résumé don't know what 98% of them do. I get résumés every day from candidates who write down ACME INC. 2009—present and never explain what Acme Inc. *does*. So, make it really clear, if it's not obvious, in parentheses next to the name of the company what the company does.

Then make the title of what you did very clear in terms that anybody can understand. A title of *Analyst I* can mean hundreds of different things. Change the title on your résumé if you have to make it clear what you've done. Sometimes candidates say to me, "Well, that's what my title was." Okay, fine, put it down if you want to, but if people don't understand what the hell an

Analyst I is, you're screwed. I've had numerous candidates over the years who had titles like *customer advocate, customer liaison, client specialist* and a few other esoteric inventive titles that really meant "customer service." So, in writing a résumé, simply write the title "customer service."

Last, and probably most important, right down how you performed in as many concrete terms as possible. Remember, *stories sell and numbers tell.* If there's any way, put in your résumé statistics or some kind of figures—that you bold—so they jump out at people. Increased profits 23%. Decreased department costs 10%. Was 120% of Sales quota. Decreased turnover 12%...The more you can express your performance in measurable terms, the better off you are.

The statement you are making with your résumé is this: *Here is who I've worked for. Here is how long I worked for them. Here is exactly what I've done. And here has been my performance. I am an excellent employee and what I've done for them is what I can do for you!*

And, by the way, your résumé needs to be in chronological order. Ninety-five percent of functional résumés (the kind that have paragraphs about all of the things you've done and then the list of who you worked for at the very bottom) get pitched before they get scanned.

If a résumé "scanner" likes what they see, they simply pick up the phone and call you about an appointment. That is exactly what you want them to do.

29. FORGET OBJECTIVES AND PROFESSIONAL SUMMARIES.

I've received résumés that have had both "objectives" and "professional summaries" that go on for two pages. Not only do these things not get read, but when they take up 1½ or two pages, it's certain that résumé gets deleted. Employers and hiring authorities don't care what your *objective* is. They don't care about what your goals or objectives are. They don't care what you want. They care about *what they want*.

Most objectives describe what the candidate wants. They are usually written with global language that means nothing. They don't get read by a hiring authority and if they do, most of the time, it will eliminate the candidate. What you want should have nothing to do with your résumé. Go look at the objectives on most résumés. You'll see what I mean.

The same is true with *professional summaries*. They do not tell the people looking at your résumé what you can do for them *today*. Most summaries are so broad and general or so nonspecific, they don't mean anything. Most hiring authorities skip them. I received a résumé a few years ago and it had a "professional summary." Part of what the summary said was that the candidate had been the "#1 salesperson in the U.S." It turned out that he had earned that honor 13 years earlier. It didn't mean a darn thing at that present time.

Notes about your accomplishments and successes should be highlighted under the particular job of which the success was realized. They should be associated with the specific companies you have worked for. They are only meaningful in the context of a particular job.

30. DON'T WASTE YOUR TIME WITH COVER LETTERS.

We did a study a number of years ago with some of our hiring authorities. Ninety-eight percent of them said that they didn't even waste their time reading cover letters before they reviewed the résumé. Interestingly, many of them said that they read the cover letter *after* they became interested in the résumé. We recently took a quick poll of some of our hiring authorities and found out that what we found the first time is still true today. People only seem to read cover letters, if at all, if they are interested in the candidate's résumé.

So, there's no real reason to send a cover letter. This is especially true when you email a résumé. Whoever's opening your documents is going to look at the résumé first. Maybe you would have a sentence or two, maybe three on the email (examples above) that encourage the person reviewing your résumé to open up the résumé. But that is all you need. Crafting a magnificent cover letter is a waste of time. Do it if you want, but it doesn't matter.

(I recently read an article on the internet called "4 Cover Letter Trends." It was written by someone who never found anybody a job.)

31. BE VERY SPECIFIC AND QUANTIFY WHAT YOU'VE DONE.

In everything you do regarding looking for a job, you need to be very specific. From writing your résumé to every interview you go on, you have to quantify everything you've done in terms that just about anybody can understand. I have just picked up the last résumé that I received before writing this. I received 89 of them today and this is the 90th one. Here are some of the words in the first *three* paragraphs, which, by the way, take up the first one-half of the page:

Training, monitoring, leading, effective, maintaining, exemplary communications, inspired, intelligent, uncanny ability, best-of-breed, creative (that word appears three times), great listener, articulate, honed written and communication styles, tenacious, consultative, results-oriented, leader, problem solver, mentor, successful, driver.

Not one word about quantifiable performance. I mentioned above about how "stories sell and numbers tell." In a résumé, or any written communications regarding your job search, you need to provide quantifiable performance with numbers. In interviews you need to communicate quantifiable performance by using short stories and numbers.

If you're going to use the word "effective," you need to explain *how* effective—percentage of quota performance... percentage of savings...percentage of increase in profits. Numbers, numbers, numbers. When you get to the interview, if you're going to tell people you are "creative," you best have three or four concrete stories that demonstrate your creativity.

32. DON'T LIE.

Oh, my goodness! This is soooooo sad.

A candidate I placed a number of years ago started his new job. Everybody was happy. The company finally got around to checking his background and found that he lied about having a degree. They fired him on the spot.

Every month, we have at least two or three candidates who are either fired or have their offers rescinded because the client company dug into their background and found something that was either a cover-up (i.e., a job they didn't have on their résumé, usually a short one) or an outright lie (such as degrees, dates of employment, and so on).

Since 1973, I have never understood why people lie, especially about something so easy to check as a degree. You either have one or you don't, and it's so easy to discover one way or the other. There are also so many services that can dig into a person's background and find literally *all* of the places they have worked even if they aren't on their résumé. (I had a candidate tell me one time that he *really* had graduated from the University of Oklahoma, but that the reason they didn't have a record of his degree is that the registrar's office had burned down. I'm not sure which is dumber, the lie or the story.)

DON'T LIE. It is dumb, dumb, dumb.

33. AVOID TIME-WASTERS.

Throughout your whole job search, especially if you are looking for a job full-time, you may find yourself wasting a lot of time doing things that don't really make a difference in getting a job. Unless you are a tremendously disciplined person, it's very easy to let your time get away from important job search activities. People do this for two reasons. First, because looking for a job is a tremendously emotionally difficult thing to do and they don't like doing it. And, second, amazingly enough, beyond calling a few friends, they don't really know *what* to do.

Even when people know what they ought to be doing, the emotional strain of running the risk of being rejected will "overpower" them. They know, for instance, that when they wake up they need to have a plan and execute the first steps in that plan. Then, maybe at about 8 a.m., they get a call from one of their buddies saying something like, "Hey, it's a beautiful day and you need a 'break' from that job search stuff, and we need one more for our foursome, let's go play golf. Our treat!" Most people, even though they know they should decline the invitation and devote themselves to their job search plan, will rationalize going to play golf by thinking something like, "Well, it's my buddies and it is a beautiful day. I can job search after I get home from playing. It'll be 3 p.m. and I can get two or three solid hours of job search work in then." Of course, what is not thought through is the one or two beers at the clubhouse after the match recounting each hole played. And we all know two beers leads to four, and even the most disciplined among us is not likely to start job search activities at 5 p.m. in the afternoon after drinking four or five beers.

Here's the point. Every day that a full-time job seeker does not start out working the job search plan, the more likely he or she will postpone it the next time...and the next...and the next. The more sporadic people are about working the process of a job search every single day, the more likely the job search activities continue to be sporadic and a systematic approach never really gets off the ground. The whole effort starts and stops so many times, it gets depressing.

The second reason that people waste time is that they don't know what to do. But you don't have to worry about that because you are reading this book and you know exactly what to do.

34. CALL BEFORE SENDING YOUR RÉSUMÉ.

Here's a rule that will get you interviews. Before you send your résumé to a hiring authority, call the person, even if you have to leave a voicemail, and let them know you're going to be sending the résumé. And only try to send the résumé to a direct hiring authority, *not* to HR. (In fact, it's almost a waste of time to send your résumé to the HR department...unless you're looking for a job in HR.)

So you say, "How do I know who the hiring manager is?" Cut it out! If you are an accountant, the accounting manager hires you, or the controller. If you're a salesperson, the sales manager hires you, or the VP of sales. If you're in the purchasing department, the purchasing manager hires you. If you're an administrative person, the administrative manager hires you. The names of the managers in a company are all over the internet. If you do your research right, you can find out who the hiring manager is by just calling in to a department and asking around. It's not that hard.

This may come as a surprise, but hiring authorities are just as frustrated with getting quality candidates from their HR department as you are in applying to the HR departments. Look, you know how many people there are in the average company in the United States—16. That's right, 16 people. So, even though you might be sending your résumé to the HR departments of those great big companies whose names are all over the buildings, those are not the people who do most of the hiring. Figure it out.

35. DON'T RELY ON SUPPORT GROUPS.

Over the past number of years, the role of support groups has seemingly become more and more important in the job search world. On the one hand, these things have grown from being a simple group of job seekers, getting together every once in a while, to rather professionally organized groups of dues-paying people who meet, sometimes, even more than once a week. Over the past few years, these kinds of organizations can be very helpful to job seekers.

By all means, if you're looking for a job, and you can afford the time to go to a quality support group, don't hesitate to do so. But also over the last few years, I have seen these support groups become so important to some candidates they become a psychological crutch. People can get so used to receiving "psychological" comfort from these meetings that they will avoid the difficult, risky challenges of having to call to get interviews, go on interviews, and running the risk of being rejected.

How do I know this? Because every once in a while I'll get a candidate for an interview and he or she will tell you that they can't go because they have an important "job search support group" meeting. I have had candidates even ask if we could rearrange the job interview because they were looking forward to the support group meeting. Even after I insist on the candidate coming to their senses by asking which is more important, the interview or the meeting, there is often hesitancy. The reason is that the job interview is a big risk of rejection and the support group meeting isn't. Don't succumb to this temptation.

PART THREE
RULES FOR THE INITIAL INTERVIEW

You never get a second chance at a first impression.

–Will Rogers

36. PRACTICE FLAWLESS INTERVIEWING.

"Just get me in front of them," my candidate said. "I've always done great in interviews. It won't be a problem."

He blew the interview. He thought this was 1998 or 2009, when you could do a mediocre job of interviewing and still get hired. It isn't that way anymore. You have to be really good. There are too many good candidates who sell themselves extremely well.

So, you have to practice, practice, practice interviewing. You have to be able to sell features, advantages and benefits in a direct, efficient manner. You have to create a situation where you relieve the interviewer from having to ask, "Now, just who did you work for? What did they do? What did you for them?"

Don't think interviewing comes naturally. It doesn't. You have to practice. You can get eliminated so easily if you don't really present a feature, advantage, and benefit *value proposition* about yourself and about what you can do for them.

37. RESPECT THE TELEPHONE INTERVIEW.

More people probably screw up this part of the interviewing process more than any other. We talk, text, and communicate so much on our cell phones that we take conversations for granted, as well as the communications surrounding the phone. That's a problem because it's really easy to carry over those kinds of habits to interviewing. So here are some quick rules:

Conduct a telephone interview from a quiet place where you can focus and where you get good reception. Do *not* do it from your car, a restaurant, any loud places, while you are babysitting, while your dog barks at the postman delivering the mail, and so forth. Poor cell phone reception will kill the interview. Treat a telephone interview with the same respect you would treat a face-to-face interview.

Try to use a landline if at all possible. Although many people don't own landlines anymore and only use cell phones, that technology, unfortunately, is imperfect and there are lots of places where the cell phone reception is poor. A job candidate has enough problems without creating this one. If you have a landline available, even if you have to "borrow" one, do it.

Set a specific time for the telephone interview and preferably initiate it (that gives you a little bit of an advantage).

Find out way beforehand who exactly is doing the telephone interview, their role (if it's a call from the human resources department or a vice president will make a big difference), and exactly what the purpose of the call is, i.e., set up another call, qualify you, interview you on the second or third level, and so on. You don't want to be caught off guard expecting one kind of interview and getting another.

If you don't have the opportunity to know exactly who you are speaking with, don't make assumptions about the person's gender based on their voice. A "Chris" can be either a male or female and a female Chris may often sound like a male Chris. So, if it's impossible to tell by a person's name what gender they might be and if you, likewise, can't tell by their voice, be mindful.

Have your résumé in front of you as well as any information you have about the company and the person you will be speaking with. Also, have a glass of water handy just in case your throat gets dry or you begin to cough, as well as a mirror in front of you to be sure that you smile.

Hopefully, and most likely, the person on the other end of the phone will have a copy of your résumé in front of them. But if they don't, don't keep referring to your résumé to answer questions. Assume they do *not* have your résumé in front of them when you answer questions and don't embarrass them if they don't.

Be sure to research, especially on LinkedIn, the person you're speaking with. Do not take anyone for granted just because you are speaking with them over the phone.

Mentally and emotionally be ready for about 20 minutes of conversation. Be ready to "close" for a face-to-face interview at about that time.

If you know to prepare for a long phone conversation, beyond, say, 45 minutes, be sure that you've gone to the bathroom beforehand. Don't laugh; having to go to the bathroom while you are trying to talk intelligently over the phone just won't work.

Answers on the phone should never be more than two-to-three minutes long. In person, answers can be longer because of the advantage of visual and personal presence. Remember that the person on the other end of the line is visually distracted by other things and if your answers aren't short and concise, they will be distracted.

Watch out for the words of "uh-huh" over the phone. Interestingly enough, it's a lot more distracting over the phone than in person. Practice varying the words you use to acknowledge the point or points a person is trying to make with things like, "Yes...I understand...that makes sense...excellent... very good,"and so on. Just make sure you are changing these words enough to avoid sounding stupid.

Disable ring tone notifications of other calls and don't put the other person on hold for any reason.

Dress for a telephone interview the same way you would dress for a face-to-face interview. Your attitude in a phone conversation is much more professional in a suit as opposed to your pajamas and your bunny slippers.

Standing up and walking around will often make you sound more authoritative and stronger because doing so opens up your diaphragm.

38. SELL TO A STRANGER.

If you knew nothing about you and you were interviewing you, how would you interview, and what would you say? Remember this question often. So many people, in the interviewing situation, act as though the listener knows who and what they are talking about, when they don't. In the same way that people will often assume everybody knows who "XYZ Company" is when there is absolutely no way of knowing that from the name of the company, candidates often expand this mistake by assuming the people they are interviewing with understand what they did, the environment in which they did it, and so on. They end up getting eliminated because they made way too many assumptions about the people they are speaking with.

As you practice interviewing, practice "selling to a stranger." Make sure that you clearly identify anything that might not be abundantly clear. One simple example of this would be a person's title. I received a résumé recently from a candidate whose title was *Sr. Corporate Customer Advocate*. When I got her on the phone, she was throwing out so many high falutin' terms like "advocacy...benchmark...consultative...partnership...messaging." After a few minutes of this, I simply asked her, "What exactly do you do? Do you 'sell' or are you in 'customer service'?" She tried to answer in a sly way by saying, "Well, it's both." I asked, "How is it both?" And she went into this three- or four-minute dissertation full of two-bit terminology.

It turned out that she was a customer service person who, from time to time, earned a commission on a few upgrades she would provide the customer. She was doing her best to try to be perceived as a salesperson. Instead of simply communicating, "I'm a customer service representative but ready to tackle the challenges of sales," she tried to baffle her way into being perceived as a salesperson in order to find a sales job.

Keep your résumé, interviewing, and everything else in your job search simple and to the point. Be sure that a stranger, who doesn't know you, can understand exactly what you do.

39. SELL FEATURES, ADVANTAGES, AND BENEFITS.

Three times recently, I interviewed candidates with excellent track records and good work histories. Admittedly, they hadn't looked for a job in quite some time and weren't used to interviewing. When I asked them the specific things they could do for a potential employer that nobody else could, they each simply looked at me with a blank stare.

After a long pause, one said, "I'm a good worker!" What?? I asked her what that meant and after another pause she said she couldn't tell me, but she just knew she was a very good worker.

If you are looking for a job, you need to be able to explain to a hiring authority specific, exact benefits that hiring authority would get if they hired you instead of the 43 other people they are going to interview. You need to be very, very specific on exactly what you've done in the past, in terms that are extremely clear, that can carry over to what the hiring authority needs. You cannot say the stupid stuff like, "Well, I'm just a good employee. Well, everybody likes me. I don't miss work. I get to work on time" or any kind of glib generality. You have to be able to communicate the specifics: "I consistently performed in the upper 2% of the company's sales force, I consistently received excellent reviews and the maximum raises the company could offer, I was recognized by management 12 times in the last year, I was rewarded the top bonuses available in the company, I was promoted in the shortest period of time of any one of my peers."

You have to be able to deliver features of your experience and background that can be beneficial to a hiring authority. They have to be clear and concise. This takes practice. Don't think you're going to get into an interview without practicing this and all of a sudden be able to explain your features, advantages, and benefits clearly and concisely. In today's market you're not going to get three "practice interviews." Every interview is going to count. Know what you're selling and deliver it well.

40. KNOW THE RATIO OF INTERVIEWS TO JOB OFFERS.

Most people don't recognize how many interviews, on average, it takes to get a job. If you ask most people, even professionals, they speculate that it takes four or five initial interviews to get a job offer. Well, the truth is that it takes fourteen.. You read it right—fourteen.

That's 14 initial interviews to eventually get an offer that you would like to accept. This average is based on the 2016 statistics of our recruiting firm. There are more than 20 recruiters in our firm. Our average recruiter has been in the business more than 16 years (the average recruiter in the country has only been in our profession for 15 months). So, on most days, we are really good at what we do. We place professionals in sales, accounting, engineering, banking, IT, and every discipline except healthcare. The range of these numbers is 7 interviews for the people in IT to 18 interviews for people in sales.

Most people aren't aware of just how difficult it is to even get 14 interviews or how long it takes. It could take months, even a year. This number may change as the economy gets better, but you need to be aware of it.

This means that if you were a job candidate you need to take massive action to get interviews. You can't rely on sending résumés over the internet, or on friends to help you, or family. You must pick up the phone and call as many people as possible and get an interview. You need 14 of them to get a job.

Depending on the economy, your experience and background, and the part of the world you are in, the number "14" may be different. I really hope it's fewer for you. The point is that it takes many more interviews and a lot more energy and a lot more time than most people think to get a job.

41. DON'T RELY ON WHAT YOU HEAR. RELY ON PEOPLES' ACTIONS.

You better get used to this rule, because if you haven't looked for a job in a while, you are not ready for this rule. You are going to be told all kinds of things, like: "We will call you back to interview you. You are exactly what we're looking for.

You are the best candidate we've spoken with. We will definitely have you back. We will probably hire you. We will hire you!" And then...And then...And then you will never hear from them again. You will call...and hear nothing. You will tell yourself things like, "Well, they are really busy and maybe they just got behind...These things normally take longer than what they said...Maybe they'll call me tomorrow."

You eventually come to the conclusion that they are not going to call at all. Anger turns to disappointment, which turns back to anger. You just can't believe that folks would lie to you this way. And then, when this kind of thing happens a number of times, there's a tendency to become totally cynical about everyone you interview with. It can get downright depressing.

To avoid this problem, remember this mantra, "I will only rely on people's actions...I will only rely on people's actions...I will only rely on people's actions!" Then, don't pay much attention to whatever you're told. If you're told a (possible) lie, simply say, "That's great, when can I expect to hear from you?" And then, don't even think about it until you hear from them as to what kind of *action* they are going to take. It's that simple. Don't get your hopes up about anything you hear, only what the next positive action might be.

42. KNOW THE PERSONALITIES YOU ARE INTERVIEWING WITH.

Not a week goes by that one of our candidates doesn't screw up the interviewing process and lose an opportunity because they don't take into account the kinds of personalities they are interviewing with. It is not uncommon for companies to have candidates interview with a number of different people in an organization. This practice really doesn't help them find

a better employee, but they do it anyhow. Arguing about this does no good at all. I've been trying since 1973.

What this means is that a candidate needs to be prepared to interview with different kinds of personalities, and this is where the rub and the challenge comes. For instance, if you're a salesperson and you are used to interviewing with other sales personalities, you can often get away with "selling" yourself with your personality, the people you know, and a little bit of sales track record. But when you go into a subsequent interview with an accounting manager or controller, this person might be looking for something totally different. This type of analytical person might only want to know about facts and figures...none of the emotional stuff.

If a sales candidate goes into interview with an analytical interviewing authority and forgets that he or she needs to sell in an analytical manner, i.e., facts and figures, not necessarily the same way sales managers would buy, they often botch the interview.

The lesson is always to be aware of the kind of people that you're going to be interviewing with. It isn't hard to find out the kind of position the person you're going to be interviewing with has. If there were any kind of person in the accounting or engineering profession, you can bet that they are analytical folks. If they are in sales, customer service, or customer-engaging positions, they are likely kinesthetic types of personality—lots of feelings.

43. THE FOUR MOST IMPORTANT QUESTIONS YOU CAN ASK IN AN INTERVIEW.

At the end of every interview, whether it be an initial interview or a final interview, there are four absolute essential questions you need to ask the interviewer. Not asking these questions will put you in the pile of rejections. Asking these questions can make you a rock star and catapult you into the finals or even ensure that you will get an offer.

There is no doubt that these questions take courage, because they basically confront an interviewing or hiring authority with the question of "are you going to hire me?" As you come to the end of the interview, here are the questions you should ask and, as importantly, why you should ask them:

"Is there anything in my background or experience that I need to clarify?" The reason you ask this question is that there is at least 35% to 40% of what you communicated about your background that the interviewing hiring authority didn't understand. Now, they're never going to admit that they don't understand because they don't want to appear stupid. By asking this question you give an interviewing or hiring authority a chance to ask for any clarifications that they didn't get or understand when they first asked a question or reviewed your background. Don't be surprised that they missed some important issues in your background and experience.

"How does my experience stack up with what you're looking for?" The answer to this question is going to tell you if they have any concerns about your experience related to what they are looking for. It will also give you a chance to address those concerns when you hear them.

"How does my experience and background compare to the other people that you are interviewing?" By asking how you stack up with the other candidates, you find out where you stand relative to the other candidates being considered. Now, you may not get a bold answer like, "You're our strongest candidate," but by carefully listening to the answer you will get an idea of how close to the top you are.

"What do I need to do to get the job?" This is a bold, straightforward question. It is so bold that many hiring authorities will have never heard it from any other candidate. Most candidates don't have the guts to simply ask this great question. The reason it's a great question is that the answer will tell you if there is a solid chance that you're going to get hired.

A great variation of this question that really, really puts it all on the line is to ask, *"Are you going to hire me?"* I probably recommend it above all others, but most people don't have the courage to ask it. That's the reason that I don't insist upon it. Most people just plain won't do it. They fear rejection. But my opinion is if you are going to get rejected, get it as soon as possible so you can move on to other opportunities.

It's amazing the number of times when I've had candidates tell me that they took a big gulp and asked this last question and they were amazed at the respect they got from the interviewing hiring authority. They heard things like, "My goodness, no other candidate has asked that."

44. THE ESSENCE OF THE "ONE LAST" QUESTION.

One of our candidates was eliminated because he was asked this question in a phone interview: "Do you have any questions?" He said, "I guess I don't. You have told me everything I need to know." Unfortunately, this sad situation happens quite often, both on the phone and with in-person interviews.

Oh my, not good. First of all, *always* have decent, intelligent questions about an opportunity. If you can't really think of any, and you can if you try, ask the interviewing authority about themselves. "Tell me, why do you like it here at ABC Corporation? I have heard a lot about you and your success here. How have you done it?" If you can't think of any business questions, *ask them about their favorite subject, themselves!*

Second, an interviewing authority doesn't care about what *you* need to know. They care about what *they* need to know. So keep that phrase out of the conversation. So you say to yourself, "Damn, that is really picky!" You are right; it is even unfair. What is even more sad about this particular situation is that our candidate was exceptionally qualified—a top performer.

In this market, where companies and the hiring authorities in them think that there are hordes of quality candidates available (there *are* hordes, but not necessarily qualified), you have to interview almost perfectly. Every interview guide and coach teaches you to have one or two questions to ask. Our candidate had been one of our client's top competitors. He could have asked a dozen questions. He thought he had done so well on the interview that he didn't have to ask any questions. Very sad.

45. BE READY FOR HITTING THE 90- TO 120-DAY "WALL."

This is especially the case for people who have, all of a sudden, found themselves without a job and have to look for a job full-time. Oftentimes, job seekers who lose their job and even people who know they need to leave the job they have get an almost euphoric idea like, "Well, you know, that was a lousy job, a lousy company, a lousy bunch of people, and they didn't appreciate me anyhow. So, man! I can't wait to find a company that deserves my skills and my ability. After all of these years of working for a stinko company, I hope the world is ready for my presence. I'm excited about this opportunity to find a new job. It's thrilling that one must be out there ready for me. Here I come, world!"

This kind of candidate gets all excited about finding a new job and sees the need to do that as a great blessing. He or she gets all excited about looking for a job and has absolutely no idea how hard it's going to be. They start out all excited and are almost happy to be looking. They develop all kinds of plans, follow all the right steps and do everything they can.

Through no fault of their own, their job search goes 30 days, 60 days, then 90 days and, as it approaches 120 days, the candidate experiences an epiphany, an "oh, damn" moment of "OMG, this is awful. This is going to be really hard. I had absolutely no idea how hard this was going to be. Wow! This is awful. I...had...no...idea." The euphoria ends and reality sets in. The fear of possibly not finding a job for a very long time sets in. They hit the wall!

Just be prepared for this. Forget the euphoria and perceived joy of looking for a new job. Be ready for a grind.

46. THE LAWS OF BODY LANGUAGE.

People form an opinion of you in the first seven seconds of the meeting and your body language says a lot. One study from McGill University in the 1960s found that people decide to hire you, or not, in the first *four* minutes of an interview. There is little evidence to challenge that study even today.

According to Careerbuilder.com, some hiring managers claim they can spot a possible candidate for a job in 30 seconds or less. Your body language sets the stage.

Here's why body language is important. Looking for a job is emotionally stressful. Most people are very nervous when it comes to interviewing and when people are nervous their body language usually reflects their nervousness. Lack of eye contact, not smiling, a weak handshake, and poor posture, along with other issues we will address here, can kill an interview. It will eliminate you as a candidate no matter how good your talent, experience or professional abilities might be.

Here is a primer on candidate body language:

- Prepare yourself before you walk in the door for an interview. Stand up straight, with your shoulders back, head held high, with a smile on your face. Blow your nose, adjust your apparel, touch up your makeup or hair, and silence your cell phone and put it away. Raise your eyebrows to widen your eyes, make you look more awake, and give you a friendlier expression. This expression and body posture tells your audience you are confident and comfortable with what you're selling—YOU.
- Look people in the eye and smile with your eyes. This means from the receptionist or assistant who greets you, to the hiring authority and anyone else you may be introduced to. A helpful way to make eye contact is to take note of the other person's eye color. It will help you stay focused and engaged.
- Keep your eyes focused on theirs in a friendly manner, "smiling" with your eyes. Staring at them blankly will make you appear "distant" and not present in the moment. If you look down, you'll seem submissive or dishonest. Looking around the room or away from them will make you come across as nervous and uninterested.

- You must initiate a great handshake. The handshake is the most familiar and traditional of business gestures and makes a lasting impression. You develop an immediate and positive connection with someone from touching their hands.
- Step forward slightly and reach out *your* hand to the other person, with your palm facing sideways. Make sure you make full contact with the web of your hand to the other person's hand. Press firmly in the handshake to "affirm" the gesture as being genuine. Shake with your right hand and, if your left hand is empty, touch the other's right arm with it to reaffirm the sincerity of the gesture. Keep that smile on your face while maintaining the eye and hand contact.
- Introduce yourself by name if this is your first meeting. Follow that by saying, "It's great to meet you" or "I'm so glad to be here, thanks so much for seeing me." It's not recommended you hug them, no matter how well you know them.
- Hold the other person's hand a second longer than you normally would. This conveys additional sincerity and quite literally "hones" the other person's attention when you exchange greetings. Honor their personal space by keeping a distance of a minimum of 20 inches between the two of you. Don't lose hand contact during the introduction. If your palms are sweaty, wipe them off right before you meet the other person. If you shake with a "limp grip" you'll be perceived as indecisive or weak. Shake with firmness and confidence.
- Proper upper body posture is essential to making a good impression. Position your shoulders and torso

toward the interviewer. Good posture has you appear interested, engaged, and ready to interact and will most likely compel the interviewer to mirror you.

- Orienting your body away from someone conveys detachment or disengagement, regardless of the words spoken. Facing your body towards the door assumes you can't wait to get out of there.

- Sit up straight, with shoulders back, and torso squarely faced toward the other person. Lean slightly forward in the chair to show eagerness and attention.

- Don't slouch down as it will have you appear disinterested or unprepared. If you recline with your shoulders back against the chair and your legs outstretched or crossed in front of you, you'll appear too relaxed and lazy. Whatever you do, don't lean back with your hands behind your head. It's a sign of arrogance.

- Demonstrate confidence, openness, and enthusiasm with correct hand gestures and arm positioning. The way your arms are positioned says a lot about your state of mind and attitude. The right hand gestures convey much of what you are trying to convey to the interviewer. Let your hands help you express feelings, needs, and convictions, without going over-the-top.

- Place your hands on the table, if you are sitting at one, or on your lap in front of you. Don't keep your hands in your lap or sitting on the table through the entire interview. You will come across as unenthusiastic. Use your illustrative hand gestures.

- Keep your hands at chest level or below and use moderate arm movements to help you express yourself. If you flail your arms about while speaking, you will look uncontrollable, unbelievable, and powerless. Rubbing your head or neck will make you look disinterested and rubbing or touching your nose displays dishonesty.

- Convey a solid self-confidence with the way you position your legs and feet. Your stance and positioning of your feet say a lot about your self-confidence. Sit with legs at a right angle and feet firmly planted on the floor. Stand with legs slightly parted and knees relaxed. That says, "I'm solid and sure of myself."

- Crossing the legs during the interview has you appear too relaxed. Locking your ankles tightly together or around the legs of the chair demonstrates noncommunication and disengagement. So does pointing your feet toward the door. Shuffling the feet indicates nervousness and discomfort. Bouncing the heels up and down is a sign of nervousness or overexcitement. Standing with your feet too close together says you are hesitant and insecure.

47. FOCUS ON WHAT YOU CAN CONTROL AND DON'T WORRY ABOUT WHAT YOU CAN'T CONTROL.

The vast majority of things that "happen" to you in the job search process you can't control. The very first thing that you can control is your attitude and we spoke about that in Rule 2. The Rev. Charles Swindoll reminds us that "life is 10% what happens to us and 90% how we react to it." It is still going to be hard, though, when difficult things happen not to lose sight of this reality. When things get difficult, the job seeker needs to focus on what can be controlled and not worry about what can't be controlled.

Remember Rule 3: manage the process and you don't have to worry about the result. Well, this is where that rule manifests itself. Focusing on process, the things you can control, alleviates the emotional strain of worrying about what you can't control. I can't emphasize this enough. Job seekers spend so much mental and emotional energy focusing on stuff they can't do anything about.

A job seeker *can* control:

- How they discipline their day
- Their attitude
- Contacting people by phone to find job openings
- Making lots, and lots, and lots of phone calls
- Following up on phone calls
- Writing a good résumé
- Getting the résumé in the hands of employers with "pain"
- Practicing effective interviewing (practicing, practicing, practicing and then practicing again)
- Practicing closing the interview
- Practicing follow-up interviews
- Asking for the job
- Negotiating

A job seeker *cannot* control:

- What other candidates do
- Not getting an interview when you've applied online, when you know you're the perfect candidate

- Not hearing from your friends or other people about an interview, when they tell you that you are "perfect" for the job
- How many interviews companies insist on having
- How long companies interview
- What they think of you (even though you think you performed your best interview ever)
- Why they don't have you back after an initial interview when they told you were "perfect"
- When they tell you they will hire you and then you never hear from them

48. DON'T TAKE IT PERSONALLY...EVEN THOUGH IT IS.

This rule dictates that you keep saying to yourself, "It's not personal." Even though interviewing and hiring is a personal thing, because companies and the people in them are considering you as a person, the decision makers are deciding on who to hire based on what they think is best for their business. It is a business decision. You may think it's personal, because getting a job is personal to you, but it is not to the hiring authorities.

Now, it is true that companies will rarely hire anybody they don't like as a person. You're reading that all over this book. But, if you see every time you are refused as being personally rejected, you'll drive yourself nuts. That doesn't mean that you don't analyze the whole situation and see if there is anything you could have done better in the interviewing process. But, if you come to the conclusion that you did everything you could, drop it.

Here is the secret. If you have enough opportunities going for yourself, you won't be concerned more than a minute when you are rejected.

49. NEVER BURN YOUR BRIDGES.

I presented a candidate to an employer a while ago. They interviewed three or four times. They really liked each other, but the deal didn't work out at the time. The candidate was smart and kept in touch with the employer. The employer liked the guy. They did have a more than normal appreciation for each other, but nothing spectacular.

Every once in a while, the candidate would call the employer and they would go to lunch.

The employer eventually hired the candidate, *seven years* after they first met. The employer had changed companies twice and the candidate three times.

I can't tell you the number of times that I've presented quality candidates to a perfect opportunity only to find out that somewhere in the past the candidate had "burned a bridge" either with the hiring authority or some of the people who were in the company I tried to present the candidate to. Business circles are a lot smaller than most of us think. People within the confines of most professions, especially after a few years, either know one another or know of one another through other people.

Unfortunately, most people remember the negative side of other people. Maybe it's because there's a tendency to boost our own ego when we are putting somebody else down. Whatever the reason, most folks really, really remember the negative things, even of what they hear that may not be true about other people. And lots of people love the gossip about other people even if they don't know them. Negative stuff about anybody travels fast and hangs around for a very long time. "Burning bridges," especially in haste or anger with others, will most often come back to haunt you.

I worked with a candidate a few months ago who, out of anger, one day simply walked out on his present employer. He just got up one day from his desk, yelled at his boss, told him they could take their job and stuff it where the sun don't shine, and stormed out. Two months later, he needed the job reference from his boss and the company. I can leave it with you to hypothesize the kind of a reference he got.

Lesson: never burn a bridge. Be nice to everyone. What goes around comes around.

50. HOW TO COME IN SECOND, THIRD, OR EVEN FOURTH AND STILL BE A VIABLE CANDIDATE.

Often, my candidates are so disappointed when they come in second, third, fourth, and so on in the interview cycle, *which means they don't get hired*. Fair enough; I understand you always want to try to win the job.

However, most people aren't aware that often the difference between the candidate who gets the offer and the ones who come in second and third and fourth are so small that most hiring authorities couldn't even tell you exactly the difference. They'll say things like, "Well, we just thought she'd fit in a little better" or "There was just something about him that we feel like he is the best choice." Most of the time there is very little, if any, difference among the candidates.

I can't tell you the number of times over the years that I've had a candidate who came in second, third, or fourth who eventually got hired for the job. This happens when the first or second candidate either gets other offers or decides not to take the job, leaving the door *wide* open to other candidates.

Years ago, I placed a candidate and he was not the first person to whom the company had offered the job. The first eight turned it down. He was the ninth guy to be offered the job. He took it and eventually became the owner of the company. How gratifying!

The lesson in this is to be sure that no matter which ranking you are, always be graceful and understanding that the organization is doing what they think is best for them at the time. Always keep the door open with a gracious and grateful attitude. Thank the organization for their time, communicate that you would still love the opportunity to work for them, and if that opportunity ever becomes available again, to please let you know.

Whatever you do, *do not* get pissed off, angry, or mad, even if you feel like you have been treated wrongly. *Do not* burn any bridges, even though losing out to another candidate is not easy to take. Always be gracious and always leave the door open for the future.

It's not uncommon for companies to hire someone and that person does not work out in a relatively short period of time. All kinds of things can happen and there's no sense in burning a bridge for an opportunity that may come up with them again. Remember the example of the candidate who got hired seven years after he interviewed.

So, do your best to come in first, but don't let coming in second, third, or fourth keep you from losing sight of the goal.

51. BE IN IT TO WIN IT.

Candidates often lose a great opportunity because they approached the interview in a casual, rather nonchalant manner. They do this for a number of reasons. First, they read somewhere that they shouldn't act like they are "desperate" for a job. Second, they really aren't prepared to sell themselves in the right way. And third, they think they are more palatable to a prospective employer because they "aren't really looking for a job," i.e., playing hard to get.

Whatever the reason, no matter how cockamamie it is, I guarantee you this is absolutely the wrong way to approach any job interview. You better go after every job interview like it was the last one on earth. You don't have to take the job if you get the offer. You don't even have to go back for a second or third interview if you're invited, but you better go after each initial interview "to win it."

People have this attitude that interviewing is a "two-way street." It isn't. Until you get to the final negotiations of a job offer, it's a one-way street and you'd better approach it that way. Go after every interviewing opportunity to get the job offer. Be in it to win it!

We had a candidate some time back who was making $150,000 in the job he had. We referred him to one of our clients, who told us they really only wanted to pay $130,000 to find somebody. After interviewing the guy over two or three times they offered him the job at $250,000. They did this because the guy was in it to win it.

52. ADMIT THE MISTAKES YOU'VE MADE…AND HERE IS WHAT I LEARNED.

If you have made a couple of screw-ups in your career (and who hasn't) *don't* try to make stupid excuses about why they happened. I recently interviewed a candidate who blamed everyone but himself for all of the mistakes he had made. It was always someone else's fault that he or his situations failed, and this was over a 15-year history. Give me a break!

Hey, all of us have made mistakes, and some, in our job choices. Accept the responsibility. Don't moan or groan about them. This is especially important when a candidate has had three or four very short stints on his or her résumé. If you've had three, one-year stints, especially back to back, you'd better address them before the interviewing/hiring authority does.

Now, a person needs to be careful here. I would pick at least two of those and say something along the line of, "If I knew then what I know now, I would have never taken the jobs. Looking back, it was a terrible mistake. And that is one of the reasons that I'm being so careful about the job I take now. I can't afford another mistake."

One has to be very careful here, because, if a person states that they've done nothing but make mistakes in the jobs that they've taken, they will come across as a very poor decision maker. When you admit a mistake, spend a couple moments explaining exactly what the mistake was and what you learned. You absolutely have to be sure to explain exactly what you learned from the mistake, and it better be a good business lesson. Whatever you do, do not go on and on and on about how stupid and dumb you were for having made the mistake. Overemphasizing your mistakes and offering a harangue on them is just as bad as not admitting your mistakes.

Here is an example of how you might convey a learning experience and put a positive spin on it-"I sure made an error in judgment. Our company thought we could get up and running and break even within two years, and at the end of the two years we hadn't even come close, so we shut it down. We all learned that it takes a lot more money and a lot longer than most people imagine for a business to get up and running."

You have to practice this kind of thing until you get it down perfectly. Screwing this up can cost you the job.

53. PRACTICE GUIDED IMAGERY.

Over the years, I have provided instructions in a guided imagery session that gets tremendous results for the users. I have received hundreds of emails from users who credit the session to not only their interviewing well but actually getting their new jobs. The guided imagery session itself consists of relaxing music that becomes more and more intense as I instruct people into hearing and seeing in minute detail the interviewing situation going very well and then repeating the scenario over and over.

Their emails reminded me of how important it is for job seekers to envision success throughout the job search. That means running movies in your mind of getting interviews and performing well on those interviews. It also means "replaying" all the negative things that happen: not getting the interview, not doing well on the interview, anything that needs to be "replayed" in a positive way, and done immediately after the unfortunate result.

The majority of things that happen in a job search are *not* positive. There are probably 15 less-than-positive events for every positive one. Face it, looking for a job in today's market is emotionally and mentally challenging.

A job seeker has to be constantly "replaying" with positive thoughts and ideas. They have to "overlay" all of those unfortunate, negative events.

54. CHECK YOUR INTERVIEW HYGIENE.

I get so tired of having to remind, even the most professional candidates, about the little things in their dress and mannerisms that will kill an interview before you get started. Here are most of them:

- Perfume, cologne, any kind of smell including body odor and bad breath (you may not know you have it).
- If you smoke, dip, or chew, you stink. (So get one suit for interviews and don't smoke while wearing it. Also give up smoking in your car while you are looking for a job. The stench gets on your clothes.) Yes! We have had dozens of candidates over the past few years who were not hired because they smoked. By the way, that is perfectly legal.
- Dandruff, dirty hair, hair in the face, facial hair (especially beards). I don't care if your wife or girlfriend thinks it looks good on you, or that you have had it for umpteen years. Grow it back after you get hired. Also: five o'clock shadow facial stubble (that you think makes you look like Brad Pitt but only makes you look stupid), toupees, beehive hairdos, or ridiculous hairstyles.
- Butt cracks, baggy pants, cleavage.
- Gold chains (for men, especially with that little gold nugget on it), overwhelming jewelry (for women, long, dangling or big-ringed earrings, gaudy, overdone necklaces), gold or silver or diamond studs in ridiculous places such as noses, lips, eyebrows, tongues, and so forth, thumb rings, lapel pins that might offend, political buttons, big watches, more than one conservative ring on the fingers ($25,000

diamond rings on your finger communicate "I don't have to work").

- Sunglasses or dark glasses that supposedly lighten inside (but don't).
- Open-collared shirts (for men) unbuttoned more than one button, loud-colored shirts or blouses, sports coats or suits or dresses or pants or slacks that are way too small, such as ones purchased 20 pounds ago.
- Shorts, short skirts above the knee, tight skirts, short pants, anything other than a suit, casual clothes (some of us remember jumpsuits).
- Ties with patterns of guns, golf, bird, dog, fish, animal, or brightly colored ties, or an untied tie.
- No hose (for women), no socks (for men), any kind of informal footwear, sandals, platform heels, boots (even if it is cold or snowing), any color of business footwear other than black or dark brown, scuffed shoes, obviously old shoes, stockings with ridiculous patterns, socks with ridiculous patterns.
- Black, dark red, or ridiculously colored fingernail polish, or decals on the fingernails.
- Tattoos, stomach protruding over the belt, no bra or revealing bra, sundresses, strapless dresses, ridiculously big belt buckles.

Please don't argue with me about this stuff. Argue with yourself. If you don't want to shave your beard for interviews, don't. If you argue that "it is a part of me and people shouldn't care about that stuff," it's okay with me, do whatever you want. I'm just trying to get you a damn job.

55. MIND YOUR MANNERS.

I know, you are asking yourself, "Why is he writing about that?" Well, it is because at least twice a month one of our candidates loses an opportunity for a job offer because of manners, mostly table manners.

Just recently, one of our VP candidates lost an opportunity because he went to lunch with the CEO and two other vice presidents and, to quote the CEO, "He acted like it was the first meal he had all week." On top of that, he ate his salad so fast, "He sent dressing flying onto his tie." End of consideration. The group doing the hiring was appalled.

We had a candidate sometime back who lost the opportunity because, at a meeting over coffee at the local Starbucks, he slurped his coffee instead of drinking it. The hiring authority was so annoyed he decided not to hire the candidate.

It seems to me that many generations in the workplace just aren't as concerned about manners as they used to be. My casual observation of the generations behind me (I'm a Boomer) is that peoples' table manners just aren't as good as Mama taught us. This isn't a criticism so much as it's an observation.

So, here are some thoughts about interview "meals":

- Practice your table manners with someone who loves you or likes you enough to be willing to criticize/ help you with any glaring problems you may have: slouching over your food, talking with food in your mouth, or eating sloppily.
- Try to avoid these kinds of interviews if you can.
- Never, ever drink alcohol in this type of interview setting.

- Order your food after you see what your host is ordering. Don't appear to be taking advantage of a "free lunch" by ordering something on the high side of the menu.
- Order something easy to eat, such as a small piece of meat, a chicken breast, and so on, that can be cut into small pieces.
- Take bites small enough that you can talk with them in your mouth. This means very small bites.
- Stay away from soups, chili, spaghetti, and the like, or anything eaten with a spoon or that can be easily spilled.
- Eat a little something before you go to the interview so you don't appear ravenous or even hungry.
- Remember, it's an interview, not a meal.

Don't let that interview "meal" be your downfall.

56. WORST TIMES TO INTERVIEW.

The WORST times to do face-to-face interviews, beginning with the worst:

- Sunday evening
- Monday morning at 8 a.m.
- Any other time Monday morning
- When you are sick with a fever. Other than that, go to the interview. You may not be able to reschedule
- Saturday
- The first morning the hiring/interviewing authority is back from vacation

- On your way back from shopping, dropping the kids off at school, or anything personal
- Religious holiday during the week that you or the hiring/interviewing authority may celebrate (Rosh Hashanah, Days of Ramadan, and so forth)

57. WORST PLACES TO INTERVIEW.

The WORST places to conduct an interview, beginning with the worst:

- Airports, train stations, and bus stops
- Taxicabs
- Limousines
- Sporting events
- Hospitals, unless you are applying for a job there
- Social events, Christmas parties, New Year's Eve parties, picnics, and similar
- Automobiles, either yours or the hiring authority's, especially while driving
- Personal residences, either yours or the hiring authority's
- Anything outdoors, parks, and so on
- Over the phone
- Starbucks
- Hotel lobbies
- The manufacturing plant floor
- Restaurants

Any place other than a business office is not optimal!

PART FOUR
RULES FOR FOLLOW-UP
INTERVIEW: A NEW BALL GAME

I don't assume not'n.

—Ted Williams

58. RULE FOR THE FOLLOW-UP EMAIL AND PHONE CALL

You have the business card of the interviewing or hiring authority, handed to you at the time of the first interview. Immediately after the interview, or as soon as possible, you want to email the interviewing or hiring authority. You don't just want to thank the person for his or her time. More important, you want to reinforce all the reasons why you should be hired.

What is most important is that you reinforce the high points of what the interviewing or hiring authority said he or she wanted and restate where or how you address those issues *better* than anyone else.

The email needs to be short and to the point. Do not ramble about how much you appreciated the interview, how much you like the person, or how you appreciate the conversation. This letter is going to be read, like the résumé, in ten seconds. So this is what it should look like (remember to make it look like an actual letter):

Dear Mr. or Ms._____,

Thank you for taking the time to speak with me today, regarding the position with_____. Your needs and my qualifications are compatible.

You stated that you wanted someone who has:

[Experience or attributes that the employer said were wanted]

[Another experience or attribute the employer said were wanted]

[Another experience or attribute the employer said were wanted]

I have given a lot of thought to what we spoke about. I would like to reinforce the confidence you can have in me to deliver what you need.

1. When I was at [name] company last year, I [accomplished the first thing that you wrote previously].

2. When I was at [name] company, I [accomplished or proved the second thing you wrote previously].

3. And, when I was at [name] company, I [accomplished or proved the third thing you wrote previously].

I'm an excellent fit for you and your company. I would like to go to work for you and your firm. This is a win/win situation for both of us.

Sincerely,
[Your name]

When you reinforce what the interviewing or hiring authority said he or she wanted, you need to do it in quantifiable terms. State things that can be measured objectively such as percentages of quota, longevity on the job, grades in school, stability, being promoted consistently—anything that can be measured in a quantitative manner. Make sure that you address specific issues that the interviewing or hiring authority stated was of value to them.

Once you have emailed the letter, you need to be aware that interviewing or hiring authorities, after initial interviews, have a tendency to move on to other things and don't think about the interviewing and hiring process as much as you think they do—unless, of course, their pain is extremely severe.

If you don't get the person on the phone, and most often you won't, you'll have to deal with voice mail. In spite of the fact that I have a ton of experience in this profession, I'm never really sure of how many times to call someone back when the individual doesn't return your call. My best suggestion is to call until you get the person. You may say, "Well, Tony, don't I run the risk of irritating them and making them angry and, therefore, they will not be interested in hiring me?" Well, my answer is that you have absolutely nothing to lose. After all, until you have a job offer, you really don't have anything to decide about.

Most hiring authorities don't intentionally think, "I'm not gonna call that sucker back. She's a schmuck and I'm not going to hire her anyhow." The truth is that their intentions to do what they are supposed to do are sincere, but the activity just doesn't get done. The process of hiring often just slips further behind in favor of other more pressing, less risky issues. So, a timely call, and many of them after that—if you have to—may put you on top of the list of potential candidates.

Now, after ten to fifteen days of calling an interviewing or hiring authority, with no response at all, you might wind up with the conclusion that you should pursue other people and other opportunities. Remember, don't take it personally.

Always be graceful, even if you were told "No." You never know what might happen down the line.

59. MAJOR RULE FOR THE FOLLOW-UP INTERVIEW.

Most candidates think that once they get beyond the first interview and they are being promoted to the next level of interviewing, follow-up interviews, all they have to do is keep doing what they did in the initial interviews. That's somewhat true, in the sense that you still have to interview and you still have to sell yourself. But most people aren't aware that interviews beyond the initial interview can be absolutely, totally different than initial interviews. The people doing the interviewing are different. They are looking for different things. They don't have as much immediate "pain" as the direct hiring authority does. They often see the position totally different than the direct hiring authority.

The major rule for follow-up interviews is: They are going to be different than the initial interview, either by the HR department or by the direct hiring authority. Companies do this in order to protect themselves. They "don't want to make a mistake" and they rationalized that if they have more people involved in the interviewing process they aren't as likely to make a mistake. (This isn't true, but you'll never get corporate America to admit it.)

I've seen as many as nine follow-up interviews beyond an initial one. I've seen follow-up interviews take as long as six months to complete. I've experienced interviewing authorities who communicated to my candidates that they had absolutely no idea what the subsequent interviews would be like because the company recently instituted a new interviewing policy. The point is, the job seeker needs to be prepared for a totally different experience than he or she might get from the initial interview. Asking the initial interviewer what to expect in subsequent interviews is a step in the right direction. Whatever was successful in the initial and subsequent interviews should be repeated, but be aware that the people doing these other interviews may see the world differently. Take absolutely nothing for granted; prepare for a whole new ballgame.

60. STRATEGIZE FOR GROUP INTERVIEWS.

Unfortunately, except in sales situations, the group interview in no way resembles anything else that goes on in business. I hate these things. The idea is to see how a candidate responds to a group setting. The candidate is brought into a room in front of three or four (I have seen as many as nine) people, and he or she is asked several questions. More often than not, this kind of interview becomes somewhat of a forum for personal, political strategizing among the people who are giving the interview.

Once you find out that it is going to be a group interview, you should ask the previous interviewing authority everything you need to know about the people and the situation. There is not much you can do about the group interview except prepare yourself to be ganged up on. It will do no good to complain about having to go through a group interview. Companies that use them are going to with or without your approval.

If you get into the interview and there are more than three people interviewing you, be prepared for a lot of political undertone. The people in these interviews are as concerned about how *they* appear to the other people in the group as they are concerned about making an evaluation of you as a candidate. They are watching and listening to one another, as well as you. So, they are relatively distracted by trying to look "good" in front of the other people in the group. On top of that, it isn't easy to establish personal rapport with three or four people at one time.

The best way to deal with a group interview is to get involved in telling stories that support the attributes you have applied to yourself. It is likely that in a group interview, especially if it is more than three people, you are going to be addressing people who are drivers, analytics, kinesthetic, auditory, and/or visual. The best way to deal with all those types of people in the same environment is to tell stories.

You see in rule #61 how important stories are in your interviewing process. It can't be emphasized enough that stories, especially in the group interviewing situation, are about the only way to be successful.

Immediately after the group interview, make notes about all the people you spoke with and what their individual questions, issues, or concerns were. Do not rely on your memory. Take notes immediately, while things are fresh in your mind. You want to follow up with each member of the group in the same way as you followed up with the initial interviewer. If you can't, try to remember specific issues that each interviewer discussed or brought up. That way, in the email or phone call, you can customize your communications.

61. STORIES SELL.

One of the most powerful strategies you can develop in the interviewing process is to be able to tell stories about yourself that prove you are a good employee and that you will be an asset to any organization.

From philosophers we learn that stories are more than entertainment. They teach us the art of being human. When you tell stories about yourself or your career, you're communicating your human side as well as explaining what you've done in the past and how you will be successful in the future with the company you are interviewing with.

From psychologists, we learned that stories are successful because they remove the prejudice of the listener toward the storyteller and encourage the listener to identify with the person in the story. People remember stories because they identify with the people in the stories. By doing that, the listener becomes more engaged with the storyteller and asks themselves questions like, "What would I have done in that situation?" When we listen to stories we get wrapped up in the drama of the story and we have very little energy left to "judge" the storyteller.

There is a study, reported in the *Journal of Neuroscience* and led by noted neuroscientist Uri Hasson, that states that brainwaves of people listening to a story begin to mimic the brainwaves of the storyteller. In other words, the listener of the story starts "thinking" like the storyteller. Using functional magnetic resonance imaging, scientists reported the neural responses of the story listeners and at the same time recorded the activity of the storyteller, and they were the same.

And from the king in *Alice in Wonderland* we learned how to tell a story when he instructed the white rabbit to "begin at the beginning...and go all the way to the end."

So, as you develop the presentation portion of your interview, make sure you tell stories that demonstrate your strong points.

There are six types of stories. This doesn't mean that you have to demonstrate all six types in the interviewing process. However, it's good to know the types of stories there are so that as you envision them and tell them you can "categorize" them.

1. "Who am I?" stories are the first type. These are stories that identify who you are, where you've been, where you come from, and so on. Stories about you growing up, working your way through college, personal challenges as you've grown up, personal stories about yourself that show you to be a loyal and quality employee are all "who I am?" stories.

2. "Why am I here?" stories are the second. These are stories about what you're going to do for a new employer, positive stories as to why you're looking for a job. "I love what I do and I love the people that I'm working for." Unfortunately, "(insert short story here)." You better make it an engaging positive story as to why you need to change jobs or why you are changing jobs.

3. "Vision" stories are stories about the future, what the company would look like if you were there based on the changes and impact you had on the companies that you worked for in the past. In other words, "This is how I transformed the companies for which I worked before."

4. "Learning" stories are stories about what you might have learned, either from successes or from failures. They could be about your own successes or your failures as well as other peoples' successes and other peoples' failures.

5. "Success" stories are about how you turned failure into success and what you learned from it. We all have those stories; make sure you have one ready too.

6. "Value" stories are close to learning stories, but they're more like examples of values such as honesty, integrity, character, "do the right thing," and so on. For example, "I learned the value of hard work by having four jobs while in college. I always had plenty of spending money and even saved money." Again, it's not hard to come up with or find. Just have a couple of them at the ready.

7. "I know what you are thinking" stories are stories that center around issues the hiring authority might have about your background or your experience that you address before they are brought up by the hiring authority. For instance, if you've had three jobs in three years, you know a hiring authority is going to be concerned about that. So you say, "I know that is a big concern for you, and it is for me too. Here is what happened. I never completed my degree because my father died and since I was the oldest of my family, I had to go to work to support the family."

These are stories that bring up issues obvious to a prospective employer, and you need to answer the concerns with a story before the issue is even mentioned. These kinds of stories take a little practice. For every risk you might have in your experience or background, you need to have a story to explain it.

Please remember that to interview effectively you do not have to have all seven types of stories. In fact, two or three personal stories about you and two or three business stories about how and what you learned in the process will suffice. They need to be short, no more than 45 seconds, and need to highlight a particular point of your career.

62. NUMBERS TELL.

If stories sell, *numbers tell*! People love to see and hear numbers. Job seekers who know how to use numbers to their advantage in their cover letters, on their résumés and especially in their interviews, always have a phenomenal advantage. People always sound more authoritative and sure of themselves when they use numbers to demonstrate their successes. This is especially true when it comes to any individual impact on increase in revenue and/or profits or decrease in overhead.

I already gave you examples of what numbers should look like on résumés and emails. Getting in the habit of "proving" your success with the stories you tell in the interviewing process with numbers really sets you apart from others. It's one thing to say in the interview that "I am/was a really good performer." It's another thing to state, "I am/was a really great performer because:

- "I decreased bad debt 35%.
- "I was 130% of sales quota this year, 125% last year, and 150% the year before that.
- "I decreased shrinkage 28%.
- "I was able to decrease payroll costs by 10% while increasing production 7%.
- "I saved the company $123,000 in inventory costs."

I'm sure you get the idea by now. You can even combine stories and numbers by explaining in this story how the numbers were reached. People will remember your story better when it's reinforced by numbers. When you have the numbers on your résumé they often lead to great stories.

63. "CAN YOU DO THE JOB?" IS 20% OF THE HIRING DECISION.

This is the most basic answer that a hiring authority needs to know. Now it may seem obvious, but you might be surprised by the number of people who make the assumption that they know they can do the job, and assume that the employer or hiring authority knows that too.

Don't make this assumption! Be sure that you make it clear to the interviewing or hiring authority your basic skills, exactly what you have done in the past that would lead them to believe that you can do what they want done.

This issue is only 20% of a hiring decision, but it is the *first* 20% that a hiring or interviewing authority is going to try to establish.

No matter how good you are, if you don't make it clear to the hiring authority how your skills and experience relate to the job they want done and that you clearly can do their job, you won't get hired.

I can't tell you the number of follow-up calls that I've made with prospective employers after they interviewed one of my candidates in which they reflected that they really seem to like the candidate a lot, but they got so wrapped up in the interview that they never really established confidence that the candidate could do what they want done. Why? They never asked, and the candidate assumed they knew that he or she could do the job.

So, be sure to establish your ability based on your experience to do the job. It is certainly fine, at the end of the interview, to simply ask the hiring or interviewing authority if they're clear about your experience and background and your ability to do the job they want done. Don't overlook this simple but important question.

64. "DO WE LIKE YOU?" IS 40% OF THE HIRING DECISION.

This amounts to 40% of the hiring decision. That's right, 40%. People really don't like hearing this. It makes everyone uncomfortable because they think that hiring ought to be more "fair" than having your personality and being liked play that much of a role in the hiring process.

But that's the way it is. It is reality, whether you like it or not. People hire who they like and they don't hire who they don't like, no matter how qualified the candidate might be.

In fact, I have seen more less-than-qualified candidates—even downright unqualified candidates—hired because they were liked more than you can ever imagine. At the same time, I have never seen even the most well-qualified candidate hired who wasn't liked by the interviewing and hiring authorities.

What does this mean? Well, it means that you need to be a "likable" person in the interviewing process. It means being warm, friendly, engaging, vulnerable, and affable without being contrived. It means being able to communicate yourself and your successes in stories that people can identify with. It means identifying with the interviewing and hiring authorities. (It sure helps to do research on these people when you are going to interview with them. Any common knowledge or experiences is always appreciated.)

Simply realizing that this issue is so much a part of the hiring decision gives you an advantage. Practice your interviewing style. Practice being "likable."

65. "ARE YOU A RISK?" IS 30% OF THE HIRING DECISION.

In all the years that I've been consulting, I never met a candidate who thought they were any kind of a risk to a prospective employer. At the same time, thought that they demonstrated being an absolutely perfect employee in every regard. What's so paradoxical about this idea is that when hiring authorities are interviewing and hiring, they look at every candidate in the most critical fashion. But when these hiring authorities become candidates, they don't seem to see the risks that *they* pose to a potential employer. They don't apply the same critical eye to themselves as they do to others.

Every candidate, no matter how perfect, poses some kind of risk to a potential employer. The candidate who has had three jobs in three years communicates the risk of being a short-term employee. The candidate who has been in their last job or company 10 years presents the risk of, "Why would anybody be in the same job, or with the same company, 10 years?" The candidate with a phenomenal, stellar track record is often considered "overqualified." The candidate with a poor track record is considered a risk in spite of circumstances that may be beyond his or her control.

Risk factors account for 30% of a hiring decision. No hiring authority wants to run the risk of hiring an employee who doesn't work out. Most hiring authorities are extremely sensitive to the risk factors that a candidate might pose. Many hiring authorities get grossly oversensitive to some of the "risk factors" they even imagine they see in a candidate. "Well, he really didn't come after the job very hard." "Why did she answer a question that way? I would've said..." "I don't know. I just didn't get a good feeling about him." "He wore a custom-made suit to the interview when we are casual here." "He didn't finish his degree so therefore he must not be a person who finishes things." "I never heard of the firms she worked for." Just the other day a client told me that "the candidate is just too perfect. There's got to be something wrong with somebody who is too perfect."

Every job candidate poses some kind of risk factor to a potential hiring authority, even if they are a "perfect" candidate. It's absolutely essential that every candidate know what their risk factors are when they go into the interviewing situation. They need to be able to offset those risks during the interviewing process with, preferably, good business concepts, even if one or two of those risks are offset by the reason that, "I made one great big business mistake. And if I had to do over again, I'd do it differently." (And a statement of, "This is what I learned from the mistake" goes a long way to making lemonade out of the lemon.)

Every job candidate needs to ask him- or herself, "In the eyes of an employer, what kind of risk do I pose?" Every candidate has risk factors. These are factors in your experience or background that might make you appear to be a risk for an employer. Even if you're a "perfect" candidate, your risk factor is that you're too perfect and they might think that there must be something wrong with a candidate who is too perfect. Most people don't see anything in their background as being a risk, when there are usually quite a number. If people are really honest with themselves, they know exactly what their "risk" factors are.

If you've been out of work for more than three months, got fired from your last job, didn't finish your degree, have had three jobs in three years, are coming back into the workforce after maternity leave or any other kind of leave, are changing careers, have a felony, DWIs, or any other myriad things, you have risk factors that you need to deal with in the interviewing process.

It's much better for you to know how to counterbalance those risk factors before the interviewing or hiring authority brings them up. Even though you've had three jobs in three years, there were good reasons for the moves. Thinking "that it was just one DWI" may not seem such a small risk to hiring authorities. This may come as a shock, but interviewing and hiring authorities are looking for just as many reasons not to hire you as they are reasons to hire you. Read that sentence again so that it sinks in!

Know what your risk factors are and offset them in your presentation of yourself. "I realize that I have had three jobs in three years. I certainly didn't design it that way. There were some unfortunate circumstances, but that is all the more reason that whichever job I take, the firm can be sure I will be there a really long time." "I realize that I've been out of work for seven months. This has been a very difficult job market. I didn't expect it to be this difficult. Although I've had some good interviews and come close to a couple of opportunities, I haven't been successful yet."

66. "CAN WE WORK THE MONEY OUT?" IS 10% OF THE HIRING DECISION.

This is the easiest of all the questions you'll be asked in the interviewing process and, interesting enough, it only amounts to 10% of the hiring decision. And it is the easiest of all the questions to deal with.

The reason that it is easiest to deal with is that if you do a good job in all of the other questions—the really hard questions—the money usually takes care of itself. Money and the discussion of money rarely end up making a difference in a candidate accepting a job or not.

Many people looking for a job talk about money in the initial stages of the interviewing process simply because it is a common denominator, and while they may not be able to define a job that they might consider or might want without being too abstract, they can discuss money in very concrete terms.

Don't be nervous about money and don't overreact to it one way or the other, but when it comes time to speak about money, approach it like you would any other issue.

Do not have any preconceived "bottom line figure" that you will or won't accept. It's more important to consider many other aspects of the job before you consider money.

Remember that money and title are the two most flexible things that an employer has to deal with and they are the two issues most influenced by performance.

Now, if you are presently employed and you have other offers that you are considering, you may have a little leverage when it comes to discussing money with a prospective employer. If you have been out of work for six months and this is the only job offer you've even come close to, you're likely to be a lot more flexible.

Try to always discuss money face-to-face. Try to never do it over the phone and don't get too nervous about it. Simply state what you think is fair after you hear what the employer thinks is fair and try to take an "we're all in this together" approach. Never be confrontational or adversarial.

And contrary to most people's beliefs, companies are not trying to pay as little as they can and candidates are not necessarily trying to get as much as they can. This has to be a really good deal for everybody and nobody should feel taken advantage of. If you take a "we're all in this together" or "let's try to work it out together" approach it will be easy and fruitful for both of you.

Practice your discussion of money with your spouse or a trusted friend.

67. RULES FOR MILLENIALS.

I'm only addressing this generation because there are more of you in the workplace than any other generation, and, at this writing, the 75 million of you (surpassing the baby boomers numbers of 74 million) are beginning to begin settling in to your careers. As with previous generations, you're going to change jobs more often early in your career (according to the Bureau of Labor Statistics) and you need to be aware of some of the issues you are facing relative to getting a job. *Please pay attention!*

Consider these traits that you, as a millennial, have and how they impact, for better or worse, your job search:

Your expertise and reliance on technology. Most of us would agree that 99% of the advancements of technology are good for business. However, in the real world of getting a job, being "connected" is only of value if you can get an interview. Somewhere along the line, you're going to have to have real-world conversations with people in an interview in order to get a job. Many of you rely on "just text me" to communicate, but you cannot get a job by texting. Speaking with people face to face, learning to look them in the eye, and expressing yourself verbally in more than 140 characters is going to be necessary. This takes practice if you are not used to it. GYHOOOYB.

Confidence. It is said that you have been raised to believe that everyone gets a trophy for participating and that has given you confidence. Well, in business most people *do not* get trophies. True that the first step in being successful is actually showing up, but you don't get confidence by simply being there. I have no problem with confidence, but it needs to be tempered with humility. As Dizzy Dean (Google him if you don't know who is) was quoted as saying, "It ain't bragging if you can do it." Let your successes and accomplishments give you confidence, but realize that your confidence will be interpreted as arrogance without performance.

Multitasking. It is said that you all think you can do this well. If you research the studies on the subject, you will soon discover that success at multitasking is not only a myth but it is actually a deterrent to quality work. Don't go into an interview touting the fact that you're good at multitasking. Any interviewer with any brains will discount you if you tell this as one of your workplace attributes.

Friends come first. Try convincing a prospective employer that your friends are more important than the job you are applying for and you will continue to be unemployed. A few years of working in the real world, a spouse, a mortgage, a car payment, a couple of kids, and the realization that it is likely that their college tuition per year is going to be more than you make in one, your friends will be far down the priority list. Don't embarrass yourself by even mentioning how important your friends are in the same breath as your needing a job.

Play then work. Common sense should tell you that communicating anything like this in interviewing situation is disaster, but I have recently had candidates of the millennial generation say things like, "So, my personal time is very important to me," and by never bothering to explain what that means, they are quickly eliminated from consideration. In fact, since your generation has a reputation for this trait, you better be damn sure you communicate in the interviewing process that work has an extremely high priority in your life.

Focus on involvement and participation in teams. Okay, being a team player is important. Everyone in business has to be able to get along with everyone else. However, you better be able to perform on your own by yourself regardless of what the team does or doesn't do. It's true that interviewing authorities are going to be interested in your ability to work in a group setting. No company wants a maverick that's going to piss everybody off. However, if your focus on involvement is more important than your individual performance, that isn't what business is about. You're going to be solely accountable for your own performance. The team will take care of itself, if each individual performs their duties well.

Don't worry about failure. You guys got this notion when everybody got a trophy whether they won or lost, but in the real world, you should worry about failing, because you're going to fail a lot. Failing to be deeply concerned about failure will keep you living for a long time with your parents and keep you without a job.

Put failure in the right perspective. Michael Jordan once stated, "I've missed more than 9,000 shots in my career. I've lost 300 games. Twenty-six times, I've been trusted with the game-winning shot and missed. I've failed over and over and over again all my life. And that is why I succeed!" Learning from your failures is what's important, but to blow the idea of failure off as though you shouldn't worry about it will not get you a job.

Respect my skills. Wake up! No one is going to automatically respect anything about you, especially your skills, unless you can demonstrate successful performance applying those skills.

Connection to parents. This trait can be a good thing, but also not so good. It's not so good when your parents continue to let you live at home rather than forcing you to get out on your own will matter how difficult or painful it may be. It's not good when your parents keep giving you advice about the job market and what kind of a job might be available to you, when they have no idea what the job market is really like. I'm sure they love you, but encouraging you to take nothing less than a VP job won't help you. (Obviously, I'm being facetious when I say this, but I can't tell you the number of times I've had well-meaning parents give advice about the kind of job their prince or princess ought to get, regardless of their knowledge of the job market.)

It is good when mom and dad insist that you get off the dole by taking the best job you can find and go to work, but the door to opportunity only opens from the inside. No employer is going to automatically love you the way your parents do. Your parents have nothing to do with the job or the opportunity that might be available to you.

I want to develop myself. There's a part of this trait that might be viable. If you begin to look at job opportunities from the "outside," judging them by how you can personally "develop," you are going to have a rough time. There might be a slim possibility that you can judge a job during the interviewing process regarding how it might provide personal growth, but most of the time, most companies aren't really that interested in your personal growth and will neglect to talk about it during the interviewing process.

Constant feedback. You don't have to worry about this trait too much. You're going to get plenty of it, especially if you don't perform very well. Your need for constant feedback, however, can be a deterrent to your success. Constantly asking your superiors, "How am I doing," is simply annoying. In the job search process, you'll get quick feedback . . . either you get a second interview after your first interview, or you don't. Either you get a job or you don't. Pretty simple! After a while—a very short while, either in looking for a job or performing one once you have it—you'll get plenty of feedback. You won't even have to seek it. After all, feedback is the breakfast of champions.

Personal relationships with a boss and coworkers. This is a nice, idealistic thought, and they can be great, if you can find them. Unfortunately, there is no way of knowing in an interview situation whether you'd be able to build a personal relationship with the person you'll be working for. That person you are interviewing with could end up being your direct boss, and he or she might be close and caring, but, like you, he or she could leave their job and the company in a heartbeat should a better opportunity come up. Don't go overboard with seeking personal relationships at work. If you get good, valuable ones, that's great, but remember that business is not a marriage.

I'll Google it myself. We all know you're independent and feel like that you can find things out on your own, either on the Internet or by asking friends. However, the organization you are interviewing with or working for have made a tremendous number of mistakes that have results in policies, procedures, and "this is the way we do things" practices. Please refrain from thinking you need to reinvent the wheel or enlighten the whole company with your discoveries. Don't be so stubborn as to not stop, listen, and learn what goes on in the company before you start "changing" it.

Feeling entitled. Your helicopter parents might have raised you this way, and the college or university you attended may have gone out of their way to make you feel special (you really were special to them—you or your parents paid them more than $33,000 a year in private school tuition, almost $10,000 a year in tuition for an in-state public college or university, and almost $25,000 for out-of-state tuition at a public college—and these figures do not include room, board, and other fees. Pay me that kind of money over six years, which is how long the average college graduate goes to school, and I'll be more than happy to tell you that you are special). To most companies that are going to interview you and hire you, you aren't special *until you perform*. You aren't entitled to a job, a paycheck, or continued employment, and you aren't entitled to a pay raise or promotion *until you earn it*. Working is a privilege, not a right. The mantra of most organizations is "If you do your job, you get to keep it!"

View work as something to be done between weekends. Approach interviewing and a new job like this and you'll get to have one permanent, long weekend.

Market myself to the highest bidder. You might also now say, "I can leave in a heartbeat, you know!" This is the height of egocentricity and solipsism (I'll save you the trouble of Googling this. Solipsism is a theory in philosophy that your own existence is the only thing that is real or that can be known). Unless you are the center of the universe, which you are not, or a draft pick in the NFL or NBA, which you are not, in this job market, you probably don't have another "bidder." Stop this silly business, take any reasonable job you can, and work your ass off.

Some of you are just beginning your career. Some of you are in your late thirties and have learned all of these lessons from the cold-hearted marketplace. The longer you're in the workforce, the more you realize that all of these "Millennial Generational characteristics" easily melt away under the heat lamp of reality. We all advance and decline in our job searches and our professional lives because of the same rules.

One last thought, which only applies to the male millennial's: you make a lot better impression in an interview if you shave before going. I'm just sayin'!

Focus on involvement and participation in teams. Okay, being a team player is important. Everyone in business has to be able to get along with everyone else. However, you better be able to perform on your own by yourself regardless of what the team does or doesn't do. It's true that interviewing authorities are going to be interested in your ability to work in a group setting. No company wants a maverick that's going to piss everybody off. However, if your focus on involvement is more important than your individual performance, that isn't what business is about. You're going to be solely accountable for your own performance. The team will take care of itself, if each individual performs their duties well.

Don't worry about failure. You guys got this notion when everybody got a trophy whether they won or lost, but in the real world, you should worry about failing, because you're going to fail a lot. Failing to be deeply concerned about failure will keep you living for a long time with your parents and keep you without a job.

Put failure in the right perspective. Michael Jordan once stated, "I've missed more than 9,000 shots in my career. I've lost 300 games. Twenty-six times, I've been trusted with the game-winning shot and missed. I've failed over and over and over again all my life. And that is why I succeed!" Learning from your failures is what's important, but to blow the idea of failure off as though you shouldn't worry about it will not get you a job.

Respect my skills. Wake up! No one is going to automatically respect anything about you, especially your skills, unless you can demonstrate successful performance applying those skills.

Connection to parents. This trait can be a good thing, but also not so good. It's not so good when your parents continue to let you live at home rather than forcing you to get out on your own will matter how difficult or painful it may be. It's not good when your parents keep giving you advice about the job market and what kind of a job might be available to you, when they have no idea what the job market is really like. I'm sure they love you, but encouraging you to take nothing less than a VP job won't help you. (Obviously, I'm being facetious when I say this, but I can't tell you the number of times I've had well-meaning parents give advice about the kind of job their prince or princess ought to get, regardless of their knowledge of the job market.)

It is good when mom and dad insist that you get off the dole by taking the best job you can find and go to work, but the door to opportunity only opeons from the inside. No employer is going to automatically love you the way your parents do. Your parents have nothing to do with the job or the opportunity that might be available to you.

I want to develop myself. There's a part of this trait that might be viable. If you begin to look at job opportunities from the "outside," judging them by how you can personally "develop," you are going to have a rough time. There might be a slim possibility that you can judge a job during the interviewing process regarding how it might provide personal growth, but most of the time, most companies aren't really that interested in your personal growth and will neglect to talk about it during the interviewing process.

68. ADVICE FROM OTHERS AND HOW DO DEAL WITH IT.

At least once a day I get an email or call from either one of our own candidates or one of our radio program listeners. They write or call saying something along the line of, "I got some advice about interviewing or finding a job from a career counselor, a résumé writer, my uncle, my cousin, my father, my brother, and so on, and they say…" And the advice is so cockamamie and off base it is terribly misleading.

The problem is, just about anyone can have an opinion or an idea of what is successful both in the interviewing and hiring processes. It's like anyone who's been married can all of a sudden become an expert at giving advice about marriage. If people have been parents they can act authoritatively to others about being parents. Maybe their advice is sound, maybe it's not.

I'm quite sure that the people who offer bad advice are sincere and don't realize that it's "bad." They want to be authoritative and helpful and throw out ideas that just aren't reasonable, viable, or true. And to someone who just plain doesn't know, there is no way to refute the advice. Recently, I have been asked to comment on these pieces of "advice" given to candidates:

- Functional résumés are best.
- Hiring managers love to give "informational" interviews.
- *Never,* discuss money in an initial interview. Ever!
  (I saw a video of this advisor giving this advice. He suggested that if the interviewer asks the candidate about money and what he or she has been earning, the candidate should not answer the question and simply say, "What does this job pay?")
- If you are a top performer, people will always find you.
- Good candidates never have to *look* for a job.
- The best candidates are always employed.
- Pay us $5,000 to rewrite your résumé and "expose" you to the hidden job market.
- Never accept the first offer that a company makes. Always negotiate.
- "Qualify" a prospective employer with an initial telephone conversation before wasting your time interviewing.

- Always let an employer know you are being pursued by many organizations (even if you're not).
- There is *always* room to negotiate a job offer.
  Companies always start out in the middle of the salary range. There is always room to go up.
- Companies try to get away with paying as little as they can and candidates try to get as much as they can.
- Interviewing is a two-way street.
- The company you want "wants" you.
- Target the 10 or 15 companies that you're most interested in and pursue them.

Well, I'm sure you get the point. And unless a person is perpetually looking for a job it's hard to know what advice is good and what is bad. But just to address the above "bad" advice: Functional résumés rarely work well. The person reviewing the résumé is reviewing 150 of them on average and they want to know who the candidate has worked for, what they did, and how successful they were. Functional résumés separate performance from the specific jobs and companies and will rarely get read. Most managers don't have time to give "informational" interviews. Unless they are your uncle or close family friend don't expect anybody to agree to that kind of interview.

If you are asked in an initial interview what you have been making, tell the interviewing authority exactly what you have been making. If you refuse to discuss what you have been earning with a prospective employer and answer with some wise-ass question like, "What does this job pay?" the interviewer will either mentally or physically end the interview right then.

Top performers are just as susceptible to economic downturns, company buyouts, and downsizing as anyone else. Good candidates are just as susceptible to having to look for a job as anyone else. Since 1973, I have heard that the best employees are always employed until those saying it are let go. There is no such thing as a "hidden" job market, and paying $5,000 to have a mystical résumé written is absurd. The succession of an offer a person gets has absolutely nothing to do with its value. If the first offer is a good offer, take it. Or, you can wait until the third or fourth one, if and when you get them, and realize that the first one was better than all of them and it'll be just plain too late. While you are "qualifying" a prospective employer to see if you want to interview with them, other candidates are interviewing them face-to-face. You lose!

Don't tell anybody you are being pursued by anybody else, unless you really are. A logical employer will ask you who you are being pursued by and if you say something stupid like, "Let's just say there are other companies interested in me," you look downright stupid. Don't lie about stuff like that. There isn't *always* room to negotiate. Sometimes there is, sometimes there isn't. *Always* rarely applies to anything. While you are thinking you have the upper hand in negotiating, the #2 candidate is getting the job. Very few companies try to get away with paying as little as they can. There are some cheap companies out there, but even they know that they get what they pay for. If they "lowball" you, don't take the job.

Interviewing is *not* a two-way street. Interviewing is a one-way street until you get a job offer. A candidate has to assume that the hiring authority has at least four or five other candidates he or she is considering. Each one of them is selling themselves really hard. The idea that the interviewing process needs to be "mutual" is not realistic. The company you "want" does not intrinsically want you unless you have sold yourself so well that they want to hire you.

Target 10 to 15 companies that you'd love to go to work for? Oh, yeah! It's *you*. I forgot it's *you*. Oh yeah, they've been waiting for you. It's a good thing they just had your office paneled. It doesn't take very long for a candidate with any sense to realize that companies don't have opportunities just because the candidate would like to go to work there.

There's a lot of really dumb advice out there. Try to get advice from folks who are actually in the trenches finding people jobs every day. Ask yourself, "Does the advice make sense? Or is it just something I want to hear."

69. PERFORM WELL ON SKYPE AND VIDEO CONFERENCE INTERVIEWS.

Skype and videoconferencing of interviews is becoming more and more popular. Sophisticated videoconferencing equipment, usually in a company's office or satellite office, are relatively professional and don't require much "coaching" other than treating it like any other interview.

However, interviews on Skype or any type of video PC network systems require a lot of warning and, interestingly enough, practice. They can be treacherous and more often than not, go wrong. I don't really like them, but a candidate may not have much choice if the employer insists on an interview in this manner. So, here are some dos and don't dos:

- Don't even attempt to use the excuse that you don't have a Skype account. If you don't have one, get one. There are other video PC programs that companies use that are similar to Skype. If you try to avoid this type of interview by claiming that you don't have Skype or don't want to do the video interview, you'll likely be eliminated.

- If you haven't used Skype fairly often, you better practice with it before the live interview. It takes some getting used to.
- Do not schedule the Skype interview at your local Starbucks or any public place. They may have free Wi-Fi, but it is noisy and a lousy place to conduct this kind of interview.
- Practice the right lighting. Fluorescent lighting has a tendency to make your face look shiny, especially your forehead and even worse, your head if you are bald. Practice with the light in front of you and coming at you slightly above your forehead. The light should bounce off of your face into the camera. Practice with soft light until you get it right. A very light layer of makeup will keep the shine to a minimum.
- Be sure to make eye contact with the webcam. One candidate told me that he put a picture of his wife and kids on the top of the computer and looked at them during the interview. If you watch yourself on the screen, you will be looking down to the person on the other end of the call. A couple of minutes of that and you will be eliminated as a candidate. By maintaining eye contact with the webcam you appear to be maintaining eye contact with the interviewer.
- Be sure to have a professional username for your Skype account. Imastud, or stilllsexy, will kill the interview before it starts.
- Make sure the background behind you isn't distracting. It should be a blank wall with a light color. Pictures on the wall or bookcases will be out of focus and could be very distracting.
- Turn off notifications on your computer.
- Practice, practice, practice.

70. PRACTICE SMILING, BEING LIKABLE.

Did you know that smiling can actually make you feel better! A number of psychology researchers investigated the potential benefits of smiling. It turns out that smiling even helps a person recover from stress. According to psychologists there are two types of smiles. There is the standard smile, which uses the muscles surrounding the mouth. Then there are genuine smiles which engage the muscles surrounding both the mouth and the eyes.

Smiling can actually influence our own physical state and it certainly influences the state of other people when we smile at them. Studies show that smiling during brief stressful situations can reduce the intensity of the body's stress response, regardless of whether a person actually feels happy. Interviewing is a very stressful situation. Smiling, especially in the beginning of an interview, encourages people to smile back at you, which decreases their own stress. (I think I've made it clear that interviewing job candidates is just as stressful on the person doing the interviewing as it is on the candidate.)

A genuine smile sets the stage for someone to become "likable." So, how do you become likable? Here are a number of things I have learned from candidates and employers over the years:

- Be respectful and polite. Especially in the beginning of an interview.
- Listen. Even to feedback from the person you're speaking with, if you have to.
- Ask questions. Especially personal questions about the person you're interviewing with. People love talking about their favorite subject, themselves.

- Use a person's name. Not often, not seldom, but just right.
- Know your audience. Know as much about the person as you can before you meet them.
- Maintain eye contact. You speak with your eyes and they speak with theirs.
- Keep an open posture with your arms and your legs.
- Be confident.

Practice, practice, practice, practice, practice, practice!

71. BEING ABLE TO DO THE JOB AND BEING ABLE TO GET IT ARE TWO DIFFERENT THINGS.

We hear that at least three or four times a day. "I can do that job. Just get me in front of them." Or, "I can't believe you don't get me that interview; you and I both know I can do the job." Or, "You know I've been an excellent performer and I am an excellent employee. If you just get me in front of them, I'll get the job."

Most job seekers simply don't realize that hiring authorities are looking to hire people with experience in exactly what they do, and who have a documentable, provable track record. There are so many qualified candidates available to hiring authorities that they don't have to hire even the "best athlete" they have available to them, as there are a wealth of well-qualified candidates who can *prove* they have experience in what the employer is looking to do.

There's a big difference between being able to do the job and being able to get the job. They're almost two different issues. Most job seekers need to be aware that in today's job market, with employers still operating under doubt, uncertainty, and fear, they're going to hire a candidate with as much experience and background as they can find. They aren't willing to take any risks.

Job seekers have no idea how stiff their competition is. They look at a job posting and think, "Well certainly I can do the job," and maybe they can, but it's not likely they'll get the chance simply because there are other candidates available with documentable and verifiable experience in what the hiring authority is looking to do.

So, the next time you see a job posting and you think, "I know I can do that job," realize that a hiring authority is looking for somebody with as much exact experience in what they do as they can get and in this market, they can find it. And, yes, even when your experience fits exactly what the hiring authority is looking for, you're competing with at least five others with the same kind of background and track record.

72. BACKGROUND CHECKS...A PROCTOLOGY EXAM.

Recently, one of our excellent sales candidate, who had a 15-year history of knocking it out of the park for three excellent high-tech firms, failed a drug test. Yeah, you read right. He failed a drug test. The company used a hair sample to discover cocaine in his body. He had reported for his first day of work and was summarily dismissed. This was the last guy in the whole world you would ever imagine to have cocaine in his bloodstream. He is in his early 40s, in great shape, and had been not just successful, but extremely successful in the sales jobs he had.

Eighty percent of employers are going to do some kind of background checks on you as a candidate. 35%–40% are going to do a credit check. My estimate is that 25% of the candidates close to getting hired get eliminated because of something a company finds either in their background check, credit check, or social media review.

There are third-party companies that provide these kinds of services to employers. The depth and the thoroughness of the checks really vary. Some of the services simply go to public records about arrest records, DWIs, bankruptcies, tax liens, judgments, and verification of a degree or college attendance. More sophisticated and expensive services dig deeper into public, as well as private, information, such as exact dates of employment, salary history, and character assessment (like interviewing your neighbors).

If a company you are applying to uses a third-party service, they have to get your written permission to conduct a background check. Technically, if they don't hire you because of what they find, they have to tell you the reason. Well, they are supposed to tell you the reason. Nine out of ten organizations, if they find something they don't like are *not* going to tell you what they found or why they are not hiring you. They are simply going to say that they have moved on to another candidate.

Companies are relying more and more on these kinds of checks because other information, such as reference checking your past employers, is harder and harder to do. Most companies have very strict policies about giving previous employment references and some simply won't do it. Prospective employers then resort to extensive third-party background and credit checks.

As a job candidate, you might as well assume that a company you are interviewing with is going to do an extensive background check, credit check, educational check, and anything short of a proctology exam. Complaining about this is useless. Hoping you can avoid them is wishful thinking. Your best assumption is that anyone you interview with is going to do extensive checks.

Ninety percent of the people with any kind of issues in their background know it. Once in the rare while, a candidate is surprised by what might show up with these kinds of checks. So, in order to be prepared, a prospective job candidate should run background checks on themselves before it's done by a prospective employer. It is essential that a job candidate know exactly what a prospective employer is going to find when they do these checks.

73. WHAT TO DO IF YOU HAVE "BACKGROUND" PROBLEMS.

Twice recently, our firm had candidates who were eliminated from contention, one with a history of DWIs and the other a history of bruised credit. The mistakes the candidates made weren't so much that they had these in their background but that they didn't inform the interviewing and hiring authorities about them *before* they were going to get offers. The challenge was that both candidates were told that, after a lengthy interviewing process, they were likely to get hired but their background had to be checked. Neither candidate told the companies they were speaking to that they were likely to have problems in their background.

When the companies did their background checks and discovered two DWIs for one candidate and bruised credit for the other, they decided to turn down each candidate.

Now, it's quite possible that neither candidate would've been hired because of these problems in their background, but the biggest mistakes the candidates made was *not* telling the hiring authorities that they had these glitches in their background *before* their backgrounds were checked. Each hiring authority felt that the candidates had not been honest with them, and that feeling overrode the issue that these problems were in the candidates' past.

If you have any kind of problems like this that are going to show up in a reference or background check, you absolutely have to tell the hiring authority *before* the hiring authority discovers it on their own.

Over the years, we have seen many, many candidates get hired even with felonies in their background primarily because they told the hiring authority *before* the background check that they had a problem in their past.

If a candidate waits for the employer to discover these kinds of things without forewarning them, the employer's trust is violated, and again, they are as upset with not being told as they are with the issue itself. The time to tell an employer that he or she may discover this in your background is when you find out you are a finalist and you are likely to get an offer once the background has been checked.

One of our candidates, the one with the DWIs, had done his own background check on himself and amazingly enough, neither one of his DWIs showed up, so he figured there was a good chance that when the company did the background check, they wouldn't find out about them. He shouldn't have relied on this chance.

So, the lesson is if you have any kind of glitch in your background, you need to tell the hiring or interviewing authority before they do a background check. If they discover it and feel like you need to have told them, their trust will seem violated and it's not likely you will get hired.

74. HAVE COURAGE...THE POWER OF BEING REJECTED.

Michael Jordan stated, "I've missed more than 9,000 shots in my career. I've lost 300 games. Twenty-six times, I've been trusted with the game-winning shot and missed. I've failed over and over and over again all my life. And that is why I succeed!"

In order for your job search to be successful, you best expect lots of "failures," failures to get interviews, to do well in some interviews, and to get offers that you want. In fact, that is part of the deal. Even the best candidates have to get fourteen interviews to get an offer, even one they may not like, and these are candidates with exceptional experience and credentials.

Expect misses. It is part of the "game." In fact, if you follow my mentorship, you realize that the "misses" are simply steps toward successes.

Keep shooting. Get as many interviews as you can. Sell yourself as hard as you can. Remember what Zig Ziglar said many, many years ago, "A big shot is simply a little shot that kept on shooting!"

75. "NO" IS THE SECOND-BEST ANSWER YOU CAN GET.

All of us would love to get accepted every time we make a call, go on an interview, and expect a job offer. We know in our hearts that it's not going to happen. As I've mentioned, there are at least fourteen or fifteen negative things that happen in a job search for every one positive thing.

Even though we would all like "yes," we imagine that we really don't like "no." And often job seekers are devastated when they get "no." But after a reasonable time of looking for a job, these people come to a conclusion that it isn't "no" that frustrates them more than anything else, it's the "maybe" they either get directly from a hiring or interviewing authority or implicitly by just plain not hearing anything at all. That's what really drives people nuts, the frustration of being told, "We'll get back to you...We will call you...We will get a hold of you in a few days," and so on. And then nothing...nada...not a word. The job seeker calls a number of times, emails a number of times, and still gets nothing. "But, Tony told me they would get back to me within a few days...They said they were going to offer me the job! And I still haven't heard anything. This is so frustrating. I'm mad as hell!"

You may not like it, but "no" is the second-best answer you can get. At least when you get a "no" you now know to move on to other things and to forget about the opportunity. Now, it may be a really good idea to debrief and analyze why you might have gotten "no." But it is time to move on to another opportunity. Drop the emotions, drop the thought...move on.

I had a candidate a few years ago who literally kept track of all of the no responses. His idea was to count all those responses before he got a "yes." That way, whenever he got a "no" he could calculate how many more he should expect before he got a "yes." The "no" actually encouraged him to keep on trying.

If a job seeker is juggling enough opportunities at any one time, getting a "no" isn't any really big deal. It means that he or she just needs to move onto the next one and put their energy and focus on opportunities where they may get a "yes."

76. SHORT EMAILS AND TO THE POINT.

This may come as a relatively mundane thing to discuss, but, especially in the job search, I'm amazed at the number of emails I and our clients get that are ridiculously long and which aren't read. Most things that are sent and received online are scanned, not read. Psychologists have found that when people read things online, they jump around a lot. They usually start in the middle of the page, move to the left, then move upward to the top of the page. They do not, for some reason, start at the top left corner of the page and read across the page like we do when we hold something printed in our hand.

The average businessperson receives 140 emails a day. Emails are opened on average for 15 to 20 seconds. Job seekers think that hiring authorities carefully read the résumés and the emails that accompany them when they send them. They don't. I've always contended that the average résumé is scanned in 10 seconds. Emails of job seekers probably get less.

If you are looking for a job, your résumé needs to be very clear and specific about what you've done and where you worked. The emails that you send when you send your résumé need to be short and powerful. I suggest no more than two or three sentences with maybe a bullet point or two. The subject line could be something that grabs the attention of the receiver and causes them to want to read the rest of the email.

I've had candidates who introduce themselves with a subject line like: "Hire a top performer," or, "Remember Michael Jordan..." And then in the body of the email they quote Michael Jordan about all of the shots he missed. It's a compelling quote. The writer then went on to compare himself to Michael Jordan. It was all done in about five sentences that could be read in about 20 seconds.

Follow-up emails from candidates often don't get read because they are way too long.

Something short and to the point like this example works:

Mr. or Ms. Smith, thank you for the opportunity to interview with you yesterday. The conversation was stimulating and enlightening. You made it clear that you wanted to find someone who was:

- *Experienced in your business*

- *A top performer*

- *Someone who has passion and commitment to their profession.*

Let me remind you that:

- *I have 20 years experience in the business*

- *I've always been a top performer and my past reviews reflect that*

- *I have passion and commitment and my references will confirm that.*

When might we get together again to discuss the opportunity further?

Thank you again,
Tony Beshara

It's not hard to be more creative with this, but the point is to keep the emails short and to the point. A three- or four-paragraph email is not going to get read.

77. TAKE RESPONSIBILITY FOR THE PROCESS AND THE OUTCOME.

I want to be kind, empathetic, and understanding. I don't want to be a right-wing, screaming fool who condescendingly talks down to people who are less fortunate, or poor, or underprivileged, or out of work and blame them for their plight. As kindly as I can, I have to say that I am so darn tired of people not taking responsibility for themselves and, not so much their situation, but how they respond to their situation.

We have become a nation of dependent whiners who want to blame everyone else for their situation and refuse to take charge of their circumstances and do something about it. Hardly a day goes by that I don't talk to some job candidate who can't find a job who blames the economy, the government, their age (too young or too old), their race, their gender, their weight, their lack of education, their mother, their father...everything you can imagine but themselves for their inability to find a job.

One particular candidate recently was Ann, a 61-year-old woman who had been out of work for three years. She had a reasonably good track record of jobs before that. She has just about every excuse I mention above. I asked her how many interviews she had had. She told me in the last year she had had one interview and blamed her not getting hired on age discrimination. One interview...In one year...One interview!

In the 40 years I've been doing this I don't think I've ever seen our society so lacking in taking individual responsibility. Maybe it's because we've become so entitled to think that everyone deserves a job, and when it isn't automatically given to them, they blame someone else. We don't take responsibility. We don't adopt the attitude that, "If it's to be, it's up to me!"

Then comes Larry. He's a 52-year-old minority with a felony. The felony is 10 years old and it involved money. Larry made restitution, but it still shows up on his record. It's certain he'll never get a job as an accountant again, but he takes responsibility for that. He lost his job as a trucking company dispatcher. He has excellent references and by the time he came to us he had found himself nine interviews. He had three more scheduled the next week and two of the nine he has been on were having him back. Okay, these are not jobs for a CFO, but they're jobs. Larry admits all of his mistakes. He takes responsibility even for his felony. The company he was recently with simply had to downsize. He isn't pissed or angry, he just needs a job. He's got a great attitude and because he keeps interviewing, he will find a job. He takes responsibility.

If folks were more like Larry and less like Ann, our country would have less unemployment and more people working. Larry takes responsibility. Ann doesn't. Larry certainly has more reasons to blame other people: his race, his age, the fact that he got laid off, than Ann. He just doesn't choose to. He takes responsibility.

It takes an average of 14 to 16 interviews to get a job offer. It takes about 100 calls to discover one opening where a person might get an interview. It takes discovering about 10 openings to get one interview. In other words, it takes a hell of a lot of work to find a job. The jobs and the interviews don't come to you. You have to look for them and go to them. You have to take the responsibility to find the job.

In most instances people don't find work because they don't take on the responsibility of doing so. Ann can't find a job because she hasn't had any interviews. Whose fault is that?

78. NEVER BAD-MOUTH YOUR PREVIOUS EMPLOYER. NEVER BAD-MOUTH ANYBODY.

Saying anything negative or disparaging about the company that you are presently with, or are leaving, is not going to do you well. Anything negative about the people for whom you were working or have worked will shoot you in the foot. If the hiring authority and hiring company have a tremendous amount of pain (that is, they really need to hire somebody or they are desperate to fill a position), they are less likely to care about why you are looking to leave or why you left your last employer. Most employers are not that desperate and they are not going to listen, especially carefully, to everything you say about your present or previous employers.

One of the biggest mistakes that job seekers make is to blame or even hint that their failures were the fault of someone else. They do everything from imply to outright disparage people they have worked for. I've known candidates to say things like, "Those guys were idiots...they didn't know how to run a company...were crazy...did illegal things...had no idea what they were doing..." I'm sure you get the message. The rhetorical question would be, "Well, if they were so stupid, why did they hire you?" (I've had candidates tell me that the people they work for were the biggest bunch of dummies in the whole world and didn't know what they were doing. Think about this—the candidate was working for a multimillion-dollar organization that has been around for almost 30 years. But, according to him, they didn't know what they were doing. Right!

I interview ten-to-fifteen candidates a week. These are professional candidates with anywhere from five-to-twenty-five years of business experience, including VPs, presidents, and CEOs. I'm amazed how often even some of the most accomplished of these folks will bad-mouth their present or previous employers. They even *know* they aren't supposed to do it, and they do.

So, unless it's public knowledge that the people you have worked for embezzled money or cheated in some way, never, never, ever say anything negative about folks you are either working for or have worked for in the past. Even if the situation was out-right terrible, the candidate can't criticize how awful it was.

The best way to deal with these kinds of situations is to begin to explain the scenario with phrases like, "Unfortunately...I made a business error...Unfortunately, this was a big mistake... If I knew then what I know now, I would have not gone to work there..." And then explain very carefully—really important— very carefully a *good* reason for leaving or why you left the company:

- "The company consolidated and had to lay off a number of people. I was one of the last to come and therefore, the first to go. I have excellent references from them."
- "The company was purchased by another organization and there was a duplication of jobs. And mine was one of them."
- "The company moved my job to another city and I'm not in a position to relocate."
- "We are a relatively small organization and I am limited to both professional and personal growth. I've gone about as far as I can go. I love the company and the people. But I'd like to find an opportunity where I have the chance at more personal and professional growth."

Stay away from reasons like, "I need to make more money... They are underpaying me" (avoid anything to do with money), or "I can't stand my boss, and he can't stand me."

79. SHAKE THE DUST OFF YOUR FEET...WHEN THEY HIDE BEHIND EMAIL.

One of the most, if not the most, frustrating things that a job searcher goes through is learning to live with unreturned calls and to emails that do not get a response. You are over-whelmed with disbelief. You just can't believe that after all of those wonderful interviews where you were told that you were the "perfect candidate" and that "you'll hear back from us soon" and then NOTHING...nada...zip.

Frustration with this experience leads to downright anger. Job seekers can't believe that people in organizations can be so rude. They go through a number of interviews that seem to be excellent, but beyond the encouragement at the end of a group of interviews they hear absolutely nothing. Even we, as recruiters, run into this—a lot. We communicate with most of our clients over the phone, but it's becoming more and more common for some hiring authorities to communicate only with email, whenever they decide the timing is best. Emails don't communicate emotion. There is very little "conversational" give-and-take. It is extremely antiseptic. Well, you and I just plain have to get used to it.

Cursing this experience and getting mad about it isn't going to do you any good. In fact, the more energy you expend toward a negative event, the more you reinforce that event's replication. Expending energy this way detracts from your ability to devote positive emotions toward what you might be able to influence and control.

The first step is to never, ever, *ever* believe what people tell you until it is followed up with by their actions. If someone tells you that you are a great candidate and that they would like to pursue you, believe it only when they follow up with the actions that reinforce you being a good candidate by communicating with you and, most importantly, inviting you back for interviews. Actions always speak more loudly than words, especially in this situation.

The second step, and this is probably the hardest, is to be as understanding and accepting of being ignored as you can. Likely 99.99% of the time you being ignored is not because people don't like you, or hate you, or think you're insignificant, or never want to speak with you again. It's vastly more than likely that they are distracted from you by other things that you have absolutely no control over and most likely have nothing to do with you. Having done this since 1973 and probably been involved with at least 100,000 interviewing cycles I've come to the conclusion that 50% of the time the company has found, in their eyes, a better candidate. In spite of what they told you, that you were a fantastic candidate and you are perfect for the job, they found someone else they thought was better. Twenty-five percent of the time their interviewing process is still dragging on and they don't have the guts to call you and tell you that they are so incompetent that they just can't make up their minds about what to do, so their interviewing process is still going on (even though they told you three weeks ago they were ready to make a decision). Twenty-five percent of the time they change their mind about hiring anybody outside the company, i.e., they move somebody from within the organization into the job (which is probably what they were going to do all along, but wanted to look like they were practicing business intelligence by interviewing externally) or they "reorganize" and don't fill a job at all, just divide the duties and responsibilities among other folks. (This 50%, 25%, and 25% ratios may not be "statistically" accurate by any mathematical study, but my gut on these things is usually correct.)

After you have sent a number of emails...with no response, left a number of voicemails...with no return call over a period of about a week, the third, and probably the most important step, is to know when to move on. Say prayers for these folks, recognize that they are "spiritual beings acting human," forgive them for their rudeness, practice "holy acceptance" (Google St. Ignatius of Loyola), drop the idea that you are going to get a job offer from them, and start focusing on other opportunities. That's it! Don't expend any emotional or mental effort on the opportunity anymore.

Keep the door open. The fourth step is to avoid any emotional response to "tell them off." Do not send some ridiculous email telling them they are rude, have no manners, or are stupid. In their hearts, they know they are being rude, but they are busy with other things. If you are a viable candidate, you never know if their first, second, or third candidate might turn them down or take another job and all of a sudden you are the "#1 choice." If you write some stupid email or leave a voicemail that tells them they can take their job and stuff it where the sun don't shine, you may never get the chance at the opportunity if a number of others don't take it for one reason or another. Always leave the door open for an opportunity to get a job offer. I had a candidate a number of years ago that was offered a job after eight others had turned it down. Twenty years later he was the president and owner of the company. You may not want the job if it's offered to you, but always leave the door open.

Here is the key: If you have a number of opportunities in the queue, when this happens you won't be devastated. You might be disappointed, but you won't be devastated. This kind of seeming insult is emotionally and mentally offset when you are involved in lots of opportunities and interviewing cycles. It may bother you, but you have so many other opportunities that you are looking at you can't afford to get lost in the "poor me" or victim syndrome. Get on with focusing on the job opportunities you have in front of you where you can influence the outcome and possibly get a job offer.

In Mark 6:11 (NIV), Christ gives great job hunter advice: "And if any place will not welcome you or listen to you, leave that place and shake the dust off your feet as a testimony against them." Move on. Jim Rohn, an entrepreneur, author, and motivational speaker, used to remind us that we have other signals these days of communicating the same feelings, but the action should be the same—move on!

Remember what the doctor says when the patient dies? "Next."

80. KISS EVERY FROG IN THE POND UNTIL YOU FIND YOUR PRINCE.

You probably have the message by now that if you're a job seeker, it's in your best interest to interview with just about any organization that's willing to speak with you. (I say this within reason. If you're a VP of sales, you shouldn't be interviewing for an inside sales position.) But, many candidates make decisions about who they will interview with based on what they imagine they know about the company, what the job sounds like to them, the level of the job, the title of the job, the size of the company, and so on.

I have candidates who I get an interview for often say to me, "Tony, I have a job. It may not be all that good a job and I may very well want to find a new one but that just doesn't *sound* like something I do. I really don't want to go on the interview. Call me with something that's a lot better than what I've got." Often times these candidates are expecting opportunities to be available to them that are totally unrealistic. As a recruiter, I quickly determine those people who are serious about finding a new job, even if they have one, and those who are looking for the perfect job (that probably doesn't exist) because their spouse, mother, father, mother-in-law, father-in-law, and so forth, told them, "You should be making more money...You're better than that lousy company you're working for, and so on." (This is really another discussion.)

My advice is, whether you are looking for a job full-time or not, you should interview just about every opportunity that you can. I can't tell you the number of placements we've made over the years where a candidate simply went to the interview because it was simply a good idea, sold themselves well, and wound up getting a much better position than the one for which they were interviewing.

As I have mentioned, you can't turn down an offer that you don't get. Go on every reasonable interview you can get. At least 60% of the opportunities that we recruiters work with changes in scope, responsibility, and money depending on the quality of the candidate and how well they sell themselves. Thirty-five to forty percent of the jobs that are "filled" aren't even advertised by traditional means. These are opportunities that sit somewhere in the back of the minds of managers, with them wondering, "How am I going to find a candidate to fill that job? Oh my, it's such a pain in the butt to try to find somebody like that, I will wait until next quarter." Then all of a sudden someone like you comes along, interviewing for one job and being able to fill another.

So, kiss every frog in the pond. Go on every interview you can. Find that prince of a job!

81. "OMG! I HAVE TO TAKE TESTS?"

First, whatever you do, don't bitch and moan to the prospective employer that testing is a lot of nonsense. In some cases, it very well is, but if a prospective employer does it as a routine part of the selection process, your opinion isn't going to matter. If you voice your negative opinion too much, you'll be eliminated for that reason alone. So, just decide to take the test in stride and resolve to do the very best you can. And, don't say something stupid like, "Oh, my God, I'm absolutely awful when it comes to tests." This may be true, but for goodness sake don't tell that to a prospective employer.

Second, before you take the test, get lots of rest, eat a good meal, and relax. Do the very best you can. Look at it as a challenge. Take it in stride. Trying to prepare for a test is hard, but there is a bit of salvation. Find out what kind of test you are going to be taking. Is it an intelligence test, a personality test, or what? You might even be able to get the name of the test before you take it. This can be valuable because if it is a test that you might be able to find online, you can practice taking it. For instance, the Wonderlic test is used to measure how quickly a person thinks. A person can buy the test online and take it... as many times as they want. It's one of those tests whose score can be improved upon rather drastically with practice. Certain types of sales personality tests can be mastered by doing the same thing. So, if you find out about the testing early enough and find out what kind of test it is going to be, you may very well be able to improve your score by practicing.

If the test is either paper and pencil or taken online do not overanalyze and agonize over each answer, nor be flippant about the answers that you give. Be thoughtful in your answers and above all be consistent in your answers. Don't try to read into every question what the interviewer is trying to get at. That is a losing proposition.

Whatever you do, do not try to outguess the test! Don't sit there and ask yourself, "What are they trying to find out when they asked that question? Because if they're trying to find out 'that,' then I will answer 'this' so they will think 'that' when I answer 'this' so they will think 'that' of me," you're finished.

Every one of these tests asks the same question in three or four different ways. No one is good enough to outguess them. Besides, when people try to outguess the test their scores are usually so goofy they invalidate the thing.

82. WHEN THINGS GO WRONG.

Things will go wrong in your job search. As I mentioned, on average you're going to have fourteen or fifteen negative things happen for every one positive thing that happens. Now, unfortunately, there are times in your job search where the wheels really fall off. You get into a terrible slump. Not only do you get two or three rejections in a row but your interviews seem to dry up and you can't seem to find anybody that will even listen to you, let alone interview you. We all go through this. Slumps are part of every business and game. Winning wouldn't be as sweet if these kinds of events weren't so devastating.

It's really easy to say that this kind of thing isn't any big deal and that we all go through it when I'm talking about the other guy. It's really hard to do when you are experiencing it yourself. Heed my warning and expect these things.

The most important thing you can do, and I really want to emphasize *most important* thing you can do, is to rely on the "system." I go through slumps in my profession all of the time. I've seen some last years, but I always know that the downs eventually create ups, and I just need to keep hanging in there and working my system.

My system and process centers around making calls to clients or potential clients. I know that if I make 200 calls either to existing or potential clients, I'm going to get to 2 hiring authorities that are going to be interested in the candidate I present. Of the 2 that call me back, only 1 of them is going to have a job opportunity in Dallas that one of my candidates might be interested in. In one week, I get 2 to 3 job opportunities. I'm going to have to send 14 candidates out on interviews, either 14 candidates to that 1opportunity or 14 candidates to 14 different opportunities, or 7 candidates to 1opportunity and 4 candidates to 3 or 4 other opportunities. My "ratio" is 14 appointments to make 1 placement. I average 3.5 initial appointments for candidates a day. You can take the math from there.

I know that no matter what, as long as I keep working my "system"—my process—I'm going to be able to place people. No matter how difficult and challenging, the numbers are always going to work for me. There are years where it has taken 16 appointments to make 1 placement, and years where it has taken only 4. I know that I can't control the economy, but I can control my activity.

83. WHEN YOU GET REJECTED.

Our candidate, Jason, was about as perfect a candidate as our client could see. He had a twelve-year history of tremendous success and a phenomenal track record. Our client, the EVP, interviewed thirteen candidates over a three-month period of time, and once he interviewed Jason, he claimed that Jason was "perfect" for the job. After three personal interviews with the EVP, Jason flew to the corporate office, where he interviewed with three VPs and the CEO, and Jason did great. Jason and the CEO had even discussed money. It was a $180,000 base plus a $360,000 on-target earnings plan.

Jason heard from the EVP the Monday after his corporate visit and was told that the CEO wanted to speak to one other candidate. The EVP explained to Jason that he had nothing to worry about, he was the EVP's choice and, after all, Jason was going to be working for the EVP.

Two weeks later, the EVP called Jason to explain that they hired another candidate.

The EVP tried to explain the decision, but none of it made any sense. There is no way anyone could explain it in rational terms. I am sure the guy they hired will do an okay job, but it is hard to imagine that he's better than Jason.

Most of the time when a candidate doesn't get hired it is because he or she doesn't interview well, isn't qualified, and so on. This was one of those rare instances where Jason could not have done any better. The lesson is that just because a candidate is "perfect," just because he interviews impeccably, just because his references are next to perfect, doesn't mean that he'll get hired.

Fortunately, Jason had read some of the things that I had written and he was involved in two other interviewing cycles. One of them was through me and the other wasn't. He didn't get all wrapped around the axle about being rejected. He didn't get pissed off that these people had "wasted his time." He didn't really like the result. He thought he was best for the job but he realized that people were going to do what they thought was best for them. His disappointment lasted a few hours, but because he was involved in two other interviewing cycles he was ready to focus on them. He ended up accepting the opportunity that he discovered on his own.

It is so easy for job seekers to get to, metaphorically, "third base" and then stop interviewing. They think, "I got the deal," and they start slowing down on interviewing. In spite of Jason's confidence in being the best candidate our client could've interviewed, he knew that he needed to keep on interviewing.

Six months later, our client called Jason back and explained that they had made a terrible mistake in the person they hired;

they wanted to see if he was willing to speak with them again, because now more than ever, they needed him. He was gracious and flattered that they called him back, but, after thinking about it for an evening, he let them know that he was going to stay where he was. He was gracious as always.

84. TIME KILLS DEALS.

The longer the interviewing process takes, and the more people who are involved in it, the less likely it is that you—or anyone else, for that matter—will get hired. There is no normal time period that is standard for the interviewing process. I have experienced interviewing/hiring processes that took 15 minutes and I have experienced ones that took 18 months, and some that started but ended with no one being hired.

The time it takes to fill a position and for an interviewing process to run its course usually depends more on the level of pain that an organization or hiring authority has than the level of the position. An executive vice president's position would probably take longer to fill than an entry-level accountant simply because there are fewer executive vice president candidates than entry-level accountants; but, again, it really depends on how badly a company needs to hire a person.

The paradox of urgency states that "every interviewing and hiring authority absolutely, unequivocally, urgently has to fill his or her position—someday." Most interviewing or hiring authorities whom you will interview with will act as though filling the position that you are interviewing for is the most important thing they can be doing; that it is their number one priority; and that they are going to set everything aside until they're successful at finding the perfect candidate.

It is not uncommon, though, for hiring priority to ebb and flow over a long period of time. (How would it appear if the hiring authority who was interviewing you said, "Look, we appreciate you coming all the way over here today to interview and appreciate the time that you've invested, but hiring you or anybody else is not a real high priority. We'd like to talk to you anyway just to see if you are a perfect candidate."?) You cannot afford to get emotionally wrapped up in what interviewing or hiring authorities tell you they're going to do. They will tell you that you are the best candidate that they have seen (until the next one comes along), and you then never hear from them again.

People in this situation don't intentionally lie—they just end up lying some of the time. You can't let yourself become overly upset or distracted by it. If you are pursuing enough opportunities, none of these things should affect you. When the hiring authority tells you he or she is going to call you back but doesn't, if you have enough other opportunities to pursue, it won't matter.

Also remember the "fear factor" on the part of hiring authorities and their companies. The fear of making a mistake is paramount in their minds. You know as well as I do that when people act out of fear, they are often irrational. So just expect it. Also, be ready for the fact that the higher up the hierarchy you go in the interviewing process, the less knowledgeable the interviewing authority is about the job you might be trying to obtain. The higher up the ladder you go and interview with people who are far from the day-to-day functions of the job you are applying for, the more likely you are to talk to people who don't know, or at least aren't sure, what the qualifications for the position should be.

PART FIVE
RULES FOR GETTING A JOB OFFER

Opportunities don't often come along.
So, when they do, you have to grab
them.

–Audrey Hepburn

If you get an offer that you just don't think you are going to take, it may not hurt to hear the offer out in total. There is a chance that you may have misunderstood many things regarding the job, title, money, or benefits. Again, you have nothing to consider until you have an offer.

If you are certain that you are not going to accept the job, it is best to tell the prospective employer within a reasonably short period of time. Also, I recommend calling the hiring authority to tell the person how much you appreciate the offer, but at this time you are not in a position to accept it.

Always try to leave the door open. If you turn down an opportunity, do it with grace and style. Whatever you do, do not burn bridges by being aloof, condescending, or egotistical. Be very graceful and recognize that you may need an offer from this organization somewhere down the line. I cannot tell you the number of times that I have tried to present a qualified candidate to a good opportunity with a firm that in the past tried to pursue the candidate and he or she had been so rude in dealing with the company that its staff wouldn't consider giving the candidate the time of day. People don't forget when other people are rude to them or treat them in a condescending manner.

If you really want to keep the door open for the future, try this: After you turn down the offer, send the hiring authority a nice note thanking the person for his or her time and effort along with a $10 gift certificate to Starbucks or someplace like it, or maybe a book on the hobby you have in common, like golf or cooking—any small gift that the person will remember you by. This gesture alleviates the irritation that the hiring authority might have over you not taking the job, keeps the door open for future opportunities, and, above all, reinforces the personal relationship that you might have established with the hiring authority.

86. GETTING AN OFFER YOU MIGHT TAKE.

Begin by knowing everything there is to know about the opportunity. Get the offer and evaluate it. If you are fortunate enough to be able to compare one offer with another, do it quickly. Another bit of advice is to never compare an offer in hand with one that you might get in the near future. A bird in the hand is always more valuable than one in the bush.

Now, if you have a job offer in hand, it is advisable to call any other organizations that you might be considering and tell them you have an offer, and you would like to hear from them by a certain time. You need to put a time limit on this. You don't have much choice, but you might ask the company that has actually given you an offer if you could have a day or so to think about it. However, most organizations won't go beyond a day or so in granting you that time. This is due to fear of losing other candidates who might be viable if you turn the offer down.

By the way, if you are going to discuss other offers with the hiring authority, in order to negotiate and compare, do it only with offers you actually have. And don't hesitate to tell the hiring authority who those offers are with. Most hiring authorities don't believe you when you talk about the proverbial "other opportunities." They consider it to be a bluff.

Some candidates, over the years, have tried to ask the hiring authority for as much as two weeks to make a decision. This screams, "I'm trying to get another offer...won't know about it for a week or two. If I don't get it, I might take your job." No smart hiring authority will grant this. I advise my clients to give a candidate one or two days to decide. Even if you are granted more than a day or two, the hiring authority is going to start thinking, "This person is playing this offer against another one. I may lose the next best candidate. I can't afford that." Then he or she will turn around and hire the next best candidate, without your knowledge. Decide, but do it quickly.

87. GETTING AN OFFER YOU WANT.

This is really easy to do. Once you get the offer, tell the hiring authority that you would like to come in and personally discuss the offer face-to-face. The only word of caution I might give you in this situation is to not shut down the interviewing process with any other organization until you are sure of the offer and have it in hand. Even then, I would be sure to try to keep my options open just in case things fall through.

I don't want to jinx anything, but I have experienced numerous instances of candidates being told that they were going to get an offer and then the job never actually materialized. So, when an organization tells you that it would like to make an offer, set a face-to-face meeting to go over the details of the offer and negotiate, if you are going to, but don't tell any other organization that you are in the process or that you are going to accept an offer with someone else.

88. NEGOTIATE WITH A PURPOSE.

In general, your ability to negotiate an offer depends on the economy and your individual situation. You can get a good sense of the latitude and leverage that you might have in the offering stage by simply paying attention to what you are hearing during the interviewing process. For example, if there are few people in your profession and they are always in high demand, the numbers of opportunities that you are going to have available to you, and your ability to leverage offers, is greater. If, on the other hand, the market is glutted with candidates, your choices and leverage are not very great.

I would never recommend negotiating an offer over the telephone or through email. The only exception to this might be when distance is an issue. Now, the final offer can be discussed and confirmed over the telephone or by email, but if there is going to be any kind of negotiation over specific aspects of the offer, those are always best done face-to-face.

Negotiating an offer, and how it is extended, is done in many different ways by many different organizations, so I can't cover them all here. Some companies send offer letters through their corporate office, sometimes from far away. If any negotiation is to be done, it needs to be done before the offer is put into writing. Some companies provide an offer letter, and, once that offer letter is in the candidate's hands, the candidate negotiates with the hiring authority. To avoid problems, the candidate—once it is understood that he or she is going to get an offer—should ask the hiring authority how the company would like to proceed with negotiations.

Some companies will make it very clear that there is no negotiation at all in the offer that they will make. Some companies accept the idea that everything is negotiable. Since there is no way of knowing where a company falls between these two poles, you should simply ask for a face-to-face meeting to discuss the offer before it is formally given.

Once you ask for the face-to-face meeting, you should write down every issue that might be covered in the offer discussion. By the way, I do not recommend negotiating an offer with anyone other than the hiring authority. If the HR department insists on making the offer, you have to insist that you need to have a conversation with the hiring authority before you entertain a formal offer. It would be a bad sign if a hiring authority will not discuss a job offer with you before a formal offer is made. In other words, you want to negotiate with the person who has the greatest pain.

By the time you get to the final stages of an offer, you pretty much know what the parameters of the job opportunity are. It is a good idea, at this offer discussion meeting, to cover each one of these issues to make sure you understand everything that has been discussed and that you and the hiring authority are reading from the same page. Leave absolutely nothing to chance.

The most important issue in your negotiating is for you to know as much as you can about the hiring authority's pain level. You will clearly understand the strength of your negotiating position if you understand as many aspects as possible of what the hiring authority sees and what he or she is experiencing. If you can, you need to find out how many candidates the employer has on the final list. You need to know how long the hiring authority has been looking and whether there are any dates of impending doom—that is, a time when there absolutely must be someone in the job. Has there been a vacancy in the job for a long period of time? Is someone being promoted out of the job within a short period of time? Is there pressure to hire someone, and who is bringing that pressure on? How long has the interviewing process taken?

Step back and put yourself in the shoes of the hiring authority. Try to objectively analyze all the things that have gone on in the interviewing process. Answer this question, "If I were the hiring authority, interviewing me, at this point in the hiring process, how badly do I need and want me?" If your answer is "desperately," then you have a lot of leverage. If your answer is, "Nice to have, but no worries" or "no big deal—if I hire, I hire; if I don't, I don't," then you don't have very much leverage at all.

The first rule in negotiation is to never be afraid to walk away. That is a hard concept to understand and difficult to do, especially if you really need a job and this is the only offer you have received in some time. But, the hiring authority doesn't know that—and remember, most of negotiating is knowing how to act.

If you sense that the hiring authority is adversarial in the offer discussion meeting, you're off to a poor start. You may not be able to do anything about this, but, I assure you, if the relationship in this conversation doesn't have a "we're all in this together; let's see if we can work it out" tone or attitude to it, you're off to a rocky start and it's not likely to get any better. Most of the time, when a hiring authority comes across in an adversarial way, it's because he or she is scared.

Over the years, I have found that the best way to negotiate is to begin with this statement:

Mr. or Ms. [hiring authority], I'm really excited about going to work for you and your company. This can be a great situation for both of us and I would really like to work it out with you. Let's see if we can both work together and make it happen. I'm excited.

This kind of statement lets the prospective employer know that you want the job and you want to try to work something out. Again, the fear of you rejecting them is lessened. (By the way, you still have the right to turn down an offer for whatever reason you wish.) Studies have shown that this kind of "let's all win together" attitude is the best negotiating statement a person can make.

Contrary to what many people might think, most employers are not interested in paying as little as they can get away with paying. Also, most candidates are smart enough to know that if they are grossly overpaid for the service that they render, their employer will catch on and they may be looking for a job, again. Most people are trying to work out as fair a deal as they can for themselves, as well as for the other person.

When you write down all your questions about the opportunity before you get into the final negotiations, you should provide some kind of salary range that you think is reasonable. If you've done your research on this job, you will already know what salary range the hiring authority has in mind. But, if you haven't, you should have some idea about the minimum amount of money that you will consider. If you have been out of work for the past three months or more, you might come up with one figure. If you are currently employed, but anxious to leave your job, you may come up with another one. If you are happily employed, you may come up with a different one. But, remember, compensation is just one aspect of a job. Don't let it be such a focus that you don't take into account other important aspects of the opportunity.

If you are asked about the salary requirement that you seek, answer by saying something along the lines of, "I'm more interested in the whole package—salary, benefits, the company, the future—than I am in one particular salary figure. I'd like to know what you and your company think is fair and to discuss money along with the other benefits of the job. Then I will know what I can and cannot do."

Make sure that you know all the aspects of a job offer before you start negotiating. Here is an elementary list of things that you may want to consider when you look at the total compensation:

- Salary/commissions
- Insurance plans (both health and life)
- Signing bonuses
- Bonuses on specific personal performance
- Overtime pay
- Salary reviews
- Sick leave
- 401(k) investment plans
- Pension plans
- Car and insurance
- Educational reimbursement
- Car allowance
- Children's college tuition plans
- Business expenses
- Daycare programs
- Title
- Ability to work from home
- Real estate assistance
- Membership to a buying club
- Stock options
- Performance bonuses

- Stock purchase plan
- Flextime
- Sabbaticals
- Vacation
- Disability insurance (both short- and long-term)
- Paid personal days off
- Health club/country club
- Separation package
- Vision/dental/family insurance
- Sales territory realignment

There can be all kinds of other benefits that a company might be able to provide. I have seen benefits such as the personal use of a corporate jet; a deer blind or duck blind lease; entry fees to golf tournaments; ski lodge participation; vacation condo usage; and partial sponsorship for a race car. I once had a candidate, who, before accepting the job, negotiated time off (with pay, I might add) to train for the World Iron Man contest in Hawaii that he had entered a year in advance.

With healthcare costs in a state of bedlam, you need to be sure about the deductibles, co-pays, and limitations of the insurance program that might be offered. Healthcare and insurance costs have been some of the biggest challenges for 97% of the companies in the United States—the ones with fewer than 100 people. Many of these companies are simply dropping healthcare benefits for their employees. You just need to be sure exactly what those benefits are, especially in the case of insurance, and who is paying for them.

Candidates often jump the gun and start negotiating money before they hear the whole offer. It is not a good idea to pick out one or two issues about an offer until you have heard and completely understand all of the compensation, benefits program, and any other aspects of an offer. So, even during the face-to-face meeting with a hiring authority, write down all the details of the offer. Most offer letters do not include any of the benefits that I've just mentioned. Some things, such as life insurance or health insurance benefits, are cast in stone. However, things like base salaries, salary reviews, commissions, and so forth may have a great variable—that may not be known to you.

After you have heard the entire offer and you want to try and negotiate the salary, here is the most successful way to do it. You say:

Remember, Mr. or Ms. _____, I do want this job. My employment here will be good for both of us. However, I need to ask, 'Is that the best you can do regarding the salary?'

Then s-h-u-t u-p! If the hiring authority asks something like, "Why do you ask?" then, you'd better have a good reason, like,

Well, my last salary was (is) $XXX,XXX and I'd like to see if we can get to $YYY,YYYY. What can we do to get there?

This approach does not paint the candidate into a corner. It communicates the idea that "we are all in this together...what can we do to work this out?" If the hiring authority has done the very best they can and either will not or cannot provide any more money, the candidate has not created an adversarial situation where he or she either begrudgingly accepts the offer or is forced to turn it down. The point is that this kind of negotiation is not confrontational. It communicates, "Let's see if we can work it out, and if we can't, at least we all know that we've done our best."

When my candidates approach negotiating an offer—either the issue of salary, or any other part of the offer—whether the offer changes or stays the same, they always believe that they have asked the hiring authority to do the best they can and the hiring authority usually does. The vast majority of time, when a candidate asks for reconsideration in such a congenial way, the hiring authority does something to make the offer better. Sometimes it's a lot, sometimes it isn't, but simply asking the hiring authority what he or she can do to make it a better deal for everyone—the candidate, themselves, and their company—creates an emotional environment where the hiring authority actually wants to make the offer better.

Even if the offer doesn't change, the candidate knows that he or she has done what is possible to get the best offer without creating an adversarial feeling on the part of the hiring authority. It makes it easier for the candidate to accept the offer, as it is left without feeling as if the individual has "lost a fight." The hiring authority will respect the manner in which the candidate negotiated.

Now, you've got to practice, practice, practice these statements. When you do, you will be mystified as to how well they work. There is not a week that goes by that I don't get two or three candidates who call me, laughing with excitement and saying, "It worked...just like you said it would. It really worked. Thanks. I would've never thought to negotiate that way."

89. IF THE JOB IS WITHIN 70% OF YOUR IDEAL.

It's hard for me to recommend to you exactly how to evaluate an offer. A large part of an individual's decision to take a job is *emotional*. No matter how objectively each of us try to evaluate things, no matter what kind of formulas we can come up with, the primary difference between an individual taking a job and not taking a job comes down to how he or she feels about it. Emotions rule most decisions.

There can be, however, reasonable questions that can be asked to go along with or, in some cases, offset a purely emotional decision. I'm not particularly wild about purely emotional job and career decisions. There has to be some logic, common sense, and reason to the decision. After those kinds of evaluations have been done, your "feel" for the opportunity will help make the decision clearer. Over the years I developed a 10-question formula to help people decide if an opportunity was good for them. These are questions with simple yes or no answers:

1. Do I like the nature of the work that I will have to perform?
    Yes / No

2. Can I do the job? Is there a good balance of risk/ challenge to the job?
    Yes / No

3. Am I well aware of the company's stability or position stability?
    Yes / No

4. Is the chemistry of the people appropriate?
    Yes / No

5. Is the compensation program fair, reasonable, and commensurate with the job?
    Yes / No

6. Is the opportunity for growth in keeping with my personal goals?
    Yes / No

7. Is the location or territory appropriate?
    Yes / No

145

8. Is the philosophy of doing business compatible with my personal philosophy?
Yes / No

9. Does this opportunity build on my previous experience?
Yes / No

10. Is it likely that this experience would have carryover for my future goals?
Yes / No

My rule of thumb is this: If you can answer yes to eight of the ten questions, that's about as good as you're going to get. If you can answer yes to five to seven of the questions, the opportunity may very well be a reasonable one, but you need to think about what kind of compromises you may have to make. If you answered yes to fewer than five of the questions, the opportunity is probably a questionable one.

Now, this is about as simple and logical as it can get. The purpose of this approach is to make you think. It is mostly a quantitative exercise and does not take into account the qualitative aspects of how you feel about the entire situation. There is no way to speculate about that for anyone. But I will tell you that if you only have, say, six yes answers to this exercise, and you don't feel emotionally attracted and strong about the opportunity, you should not take the job because you probably won't be very successful. If you have a total of five yes answers to the survey but you feel tremendously passionate, enthusiastic, and have a "failure is not an option" attitude toward the opportunity, you may well be able to make it a good one.

The purpose of these questions is to help you think out on paper (or aloud, with your coach) all aspects of the opportunity. The final decision will be an emotionally driven one, but at least you will have a reasonably logical assessment of the job opportunity's compatibility.

These questions do not take into account things such as how long you've been out of work and how many other opportunities you may have available to you. If you have been out of work for six months, and this is the only offer that you have received, the number of yes answers may not even matter.

Another way to evaluate an offer is the Ben Franklin approach, which means to simply write down the pros and cons, and analyze them. If you have 10 or 12 reasons why you ought to accept the job and only two or three reasons why you shouldn't, the decision is fairly obvious. The idea is to make you think about all aspects of the position.

Forcing yourself to write out the pros and cons so that you can see all the issues is also a great catharsis. Having your coach helping you out with this exercise is certainly of value. Talking it out with your coach is also of value. Hearing yourself talk about an opportunity and what you think and feel about it will also give you a great perspective.

In the final analysis, I have always stated that if you can get 70 percent of what you would ideally like in an opportunity, it is about as good as you are going to do. Now, again, this depends on situations to which I am not privy.

At the end of the game, there is always a risk in taking a new job. Do the best you can to analyze all the factors that are involved. Then, follow your gut!

90. AVOID MANGLED METAPHORS AND MISAPPLIED ANALOGIES.

I can't tell you the number of very educated candidates over the years who in their speaking become fond of metaphors, which is okay, however, they mangle the metaphor...and misapply the analogy.

They say things like "pass mustard" instead of "pass muster," "took off like haywire" instead of "wildfire," "preaching to the congregation" instead of "choir." I have had candidates tell me they wanted to "hit the ball running," "give their best foot forward," or said, "I'm living fat on the hog." I have heard, "the cream will rise to the crop...you are barking up the wrong dog...eats at my crawl...brightest block in the box." I could go on, but you get the message. We have all heard folks do this at times. We are amused and kind of laugh. But in the interviewing situation, they can be disastrous, especially if they are repeated...repeatedly. They are distracting and, in most cases, don't reflect well on the person being interviewed. Soooo, practice interviewing...if you have a tendency to mangle your metaphors or misapply your analogies, have someone help you or get yourself some and Google a few. If you are going to lose a deal, don't let it be over something so simple to correct.

Here are a few of the latest ones I have heard:

- "As long as that dog hunts, we'll ride him."
- "It's the best thing since sliced Spam."
- "Never judge a book by its title."
- "Never put all your eggs in one omelet."
- "The guy just couldn't cut the custard."
- "That guy is a wolf in cheap clothing."

So, keep your nose to the ground and your ear to the grindstone...practice interviewing...watch the pictures you describe.

91. "STOPGAP" JOBS—FULL-TIME, PART-TIME, TEMPORARY.

This is one of the most difficult challenges that full-time job seekers run into. As they are beginning to run out of money, and can't find a job commensurate with what they have been doing, they are faced with finding a "stopgap" job. They always go out and find one of these jobs thinking that it will only be for a short period of time until they find a permanent job commensurate with what they've done before.

The problem with this is that, no matter how sincere the intentions are, these stopgap jobs can often times get in the way of finding a full-time job. Even outright temporary jobs can cause the same problem. Over the years I've had candidates, out of the need to pay the rent, take a stopgap job with the intention of continuing to interview for the kind of job they really want. Often times, however, this stopgap job gets in the way of the candidate being able to interview for the kind of job they really want.

Over the years, I've had all kinds of candidates who have taken stopgap jobs. I called them with the opportunity for an interview in their chosen field and they tell me they can't make the interview because "I have to work" or "I don't know if I can get off work to interview." Their need to make immediate money gets in the way of a long-term opportunity in a career they've chosen. On top of that, it is a tremendous emotional strain trying to juggle a stopgap job while trying to get time off to go to a career-type interview.

After several "strenuous" times of having to show up in an interview while working around the stopgap job, they become mentally and emotionally exhausted and, after a while, decline the career interview because it's just too difficult. Pretty soon they have worked at the stopgap job for nine months or so. They have then exacerbated the problem, because now, they have to explain to a potential employer why they have been so long at a stopgap job.

It is extremely hard to explain to a potential employer why you have been at a stopgap job for more than six months. Their attitude is, "Well, if this gal is so good and career-oriented, why has she not found a job in her career sooner?" It becomes a real problem.

My suggestion is, if you're going to take a stopgap job get one at night: second shift at Starbucks, waiting tables at a restaurant (making $25,000 to $50,000, hourly wage plus tips is possible), second shift in the manufacturing or distribution environment. This will give you a chance to interview on your free time in the late morning or very early afternoon. I will share with you, though, that this takes a tremendous amount of self-discipline and the ability to develop a very strict routine of working late, getting up late enough to get a decent night's rest, but early enough to be able to interview. Even people who do this fall into the trap of keeping the evening or night job and missing the interviews because they are just too tired and need to sleep.

Temporary jobs, however, can be quite different. Temporary jobs in the administrative, accounting, manufacturing and distribution, IT, drafting and design, and a number of other disciplines can often result in permanent positions. There are some of our clients who hire many people in these disciplines on a temporary basis to begin with just to see how good a worker they might be. In fact, the criteria for getting these "temporary" positions are not much different than the criteria for hiring someone on a permanent basis.

My suggestion is, use your good judgment. If a temporary assignment is about all you can find, then certainly consider it.

Sixty percent of them become permanent positions. Do your best to find a temporary job that is commensurate with the kind of thing that you've done before. Work your butt off just as though it was a permanent job. You'll often be amazed at the results.

92. COUNTEROFFER DISASTER.

A counteroffer is when the candidate goes in to resign and the company tries to buy him or her back. The employer tries to do things to patch up the relationship when the person goes in to resign. Counteroffers are a disaster 98% of the time. It hardly ever works out for the candidate.

I have seen hundreds of counteroffers over the years, where a candidate decides to stay with his or her current employer. However, I know very few who have ever lasted long at all. Nearly every candidate that I've ever known to receive and accept a counteroffer leaves the company within a four- to six-month period—either on his or her own volition or because the person is fired. And most of the time, when this happens, it is an adversarial, acrimonious departure. Once a counteroffer is made and accepted, the whole relationship between the employer and the employee who was looking to leave has changed. The emotional strain that it creates results in a distressful, distrustful relationship that becomes irreparable.

More often than not, a candidate who goes to the trouble to go out and look for a job (and actually receives another offer) doesn't really think about a counteroffer. It usually comes as a little bit of a surprise. Don't let that happen!

Here are 16 reasons why counteroffers rarely work:

1. If your company really recognized your worth, they would've given you the added income, advancement,

title, whatever without the necessity of you, in effect, blackmailing your employer by finding another job and threatening to quit.

2. If you accept the counteroffer, you will usually be looked upon as a person who blackmailed management or the company into giving you what you wanted.

3. When the next salary reviews come around, you will already have received your raise and you will be bypassed.

4. The reason that you were made a counteroffer is that, at that moment, they needed you worse than you needed them.

5. In essence, you are firing your company. No one likes to be fired. So, the company is going to do what any fired person would do: hang on until it can rectify the situation—that is, replace you.

6. Well-managed companies don't buy people back. The only kind of company that will buy you back is the kind of company that will take advantage of you somewhere down the line.

7. It is cheaper for a company to try to make you a counteroffer than it is to immediately replace you.

8. Money and title are temporary. If the major complaint about your job has to do with money, when the money changes, you'll only be temporarily content.

9. The momentary emotion of suddenly being made to feel special overrides the logical, common sense that forced you to go out and look for a job.

10. The trust relationship that you had with your employer is no longer there.

11. The fact that you can no longer be trusted affects everyone you work with. You held management's feet to the fire, you blackmailed them, and, what is worse, everyone in the company knows it.

12. You caught management with their pants down. Most likely, they had no idea this was coming. So, they're going to do whatever they can to keep you so that they can buy time and find a replacement.

13. Your supervisor and your company, at least for a while, are going to put their finger in the dike to keep you around simply because other people are going to have to take up your slack if you leave.

14. Your immediate supervisor is likely to say, "How could you do this now? It couldn't come at a worse time!" Your ego will be stroked and fed simply to buy time for your manager to recover by replacing you.

15. The world is motivated by self-interest. If your leaving makes your supervisor look bad, he or she is going to do anything reasonable to look good by keeping you— then look really good and decisive by firing you with a replacement in the wings.

16. The higher-level position that you have, the more likely you are to be presented with a counteroffer by more than one person in the organization. I've had candidates who, once they gave their resignation notice, were literally escorted from manager to manager throughout the company to convince the candidate to stay.

Put your ego aside and follow good common sense. Tell the people making you a counteroffer that you really appreciate their offer, but that you have made up your mind and you are going to leave. *No matter how tempting it is, never accept a counteroffer.*

93. LOOKING FOR A JOB REMOTELY... "BUT I'M WILLING TO RELOCATE."

I get three to four calls a week of people who want to relocate to the Dallas-Fort Worth area. When I explained to them that it is almost impossible to find a job in DFW when you're not already living here, they get a bit indignant and, especially, if they have a job, can't seem to understand that the interviewing and hiring process is so long and arduous, it's almost impossible to do when you're not living here. Inevitably, they claim that they would be more than happy to come here to interview when they need to. Most of them even offer that they will be willing to pay their own relocation, but it just isn't practical. Finding a job, even when you are living locally and have great skills as well as a great track record, takes six to eight weeks.

If you're not living in the area you are looking for work, you have to sponsor yourself coming here for an initial interview. If you're employed, you have to take time off to get here for the initial interview. If you are liked, the firm may want to have you back, sometimes the very next week, to compete with other candidates on the second round. So, you have to get to that area for a second time. Most of the time final interviews are a week or so after that, and, if you make it that far in the interviewing process, you have to come back, which you'll do if you are considered a finalist. If you don't get hired the thought of having to repeat this same process two or three times is more than you can imagine. And you decide you won't do that again. It's just too exhausting.

Unfortunately, our firm has to explain that there are more than 6 million people here in the Dallas-Fort Worth area and most employers can't imagine why they would even have to consider hiring somebody who doesn't already live here. They don't even want to consider the hassle of having to hire someone who has to move here, even if they pay their own way, and run the risk of them going back home to pack up and move and have their spouse or children convince them to stay. They just don't see the need to run that risk. And in most cases, they don't.

This principle doesn't apply if you are the kind of candidate who has a very narrow, specific kind of background that is extremely hard to find. Or if the job is in a remote part of the country and the only way that a company might be able to find people like you is to relocate them. You certainly know if you fall into this kind of category. But for most people wanting to relocate to a large metropolitan area, and thinking that their experience is second to none, they need to realize that employers in those large metropolitan cities imagine, whether it's true or not, that there are wads of candidates just as good in their area.

So, I know there are exceptions, and you might be one of them, but if you decide to find a job in a distant city, it's going to be a lot harder than you think

94. REFERENCES.

People take these for granted and at least once a week, I personally run into a challenge with them. Either the candidate doesn't prepare his or her references, provides the wrong kind of references, or gets people as references who end up costing him or her the job. So, if you're looking for a job you need to know about your references. Pay attention.

Hiring authorities rely more on previous employment references than they ever have. Even a mediocre reference can kill a potential job opportunity. If you're the kind of candidate who has excellent references from everyone you have ever worked for, you probably don't need to pay attention to what I'm writing. It may not hurt to read it because some of the logistical ideas are of value, but you may not need much help.

One of the most shocking surprises anyone can ever have is the experience of assuming all your references are excellent, only to find out that one or more of them cost you a job opportunity. I estimate at least 20% to 25% of the job-seeking candidates out there had at least one reference challenge in their background, and they have absolutely no idea it is there.

This may come as a surprise, but except in instances of disclosing acts of violence or acts of financial mismanagement, companies are not legally required to provide any kind of reference about previous employees. Companies may be subject to a charge of defamation by giving a reference that can be construed as bad and they have absolutely nothing to gain by giving any kind of a reference, good or bad. Any kind of reference an organization will provide goes beyond what they have to do.

Companies will usually verify dates of employment, earnings, and confirm if a person is eligible for rehire in the eyes of the company, but there is nothing that says they have to do any of this. Many companies will not even respond to references solicited over the phone. They require a written request for most references and only respond to those requests in writing.

Most prospective employers are going to ask you for specific references from the most recent jobs you had. Even in situations where you know the previous company is not going to provide an adequate reference, it is going to be difficult to find someone within the company who can speak of your performance if it's against the policies of the company, and this poses a tremendous difficulty for many candidates.

Most employers will ask you to give them three or four people as references and specify the relationship you had with those people. Some employers are going to ask you for specific people, like previous supervisors, customers, or maybe, peers. Be sure you're prepared to provide these different kinds of references when asked.

As you begin your job search, it is a good idea to think about who you might give as a reference in just about any interviewing process. I would recommend calling those people to let them know you're actively looking for a position, and ask their permission to use them as a reference. It is very rare, but I've seen situations where the people who candidates thought would be a reference for them refused to do it. After they give you permission, inform them you will let them know who might be checking your reference, what kind of position it is, what kind of employer they are, what kinds of things they are going to ask, and exactly what in your background he or she should emphasize when the reference is checked.

There's nothing more disastrous than an unprepared reference who tells the hiring authority something totally different about the candidate than the candidate has told the interviewing hiring authority. It is not that the reference would lie, but references will often reinforce experience and traits about a previous employee that had nothing to do with the job the employee is interviewing for. If you brief your reference correctly, they will anticipate questions that will be asked and give answers that will help you get the job.

As long as we are talking about references, I want to mention something that happened recently and which happens a number of times a year; it's a great lesson of what not to do.

Do not put your references on your résumé. We had a candidate who listed his references on his résumé. He sent the résumé into a prospective employer (not our client) and the employer liked the résumé and the places the person had worked.

Instead of calling a candidate for an interview, however, the hiring authority called two of the candidate's references and invited them in for an interview. The candidate had not only put the names of his references on his résumé, but also their titles and phone numbers. One of the references called the candidate and actually told him how he had gotten the interview. The candidate was not very happy. He mentioned to us he thought it was very unethical for a hiring authority to do this kind of thing.

It is nothing of the sort. The hiring authority is trying to find the best candidate possible, any way possible.

95. THE LAW OF INATTENTIONAL BLINDNESS.

Daniel J. Simons is a professor of psychology at the University of Illinois. He studies human attention, perception, and memory. In nearly every study he has ever conducted, he has discovered that most of our skills regarding attention, perception, and memory are nowhere as good as we think. His most famous study was conducted in 1999. He asked subjects to view a video of six people passing two basketballs back and forth. The subjects were asked to count the number of times three players wearing white shirts passed the basketball while ignoring the players wearing black who passed their own ball. After a few passes a person wearing a gorilla suit expectantly walks through the scene. 50% of subjects failed to notice the person in the gorilla suit. (You can find this video on YouTube.)

Simons proves the theory that there is a big mismatch between what we see and what we think we see. This condition is called "inattentional blindness." He has even tested the effects of this in real-world conditions. Subjects were asked to follow an experimenter on the back of a truck while they were jogging. While jogging, they were to monitor how many times the experimenter touched his hat. As they were jogging along a predefined route, they ran past a simulated fight scene in which two other experimenters were "beating" a victim. The researchers found that even in broad daylight, only 56% of the subjects noticed the fight.

The lesson is that people see about what they want to see and forget to look at the rest. This applies to the interviewing and hiring process more than most people will ever admit. Employers especially will get hung up on one or two issues in a candidate's background –sometimes for better or for worse— and disregard or don't pay attention to other aspects of it. One prime example of this is the candidate who had three jobs in the last two years. The vast majority of employers are going to get hung up on that fact and hardly go beyond it to delve into a candidate's experience or performance. They simply stop and move on to another candidate. Candidates often do the same thing when they consider looking at a company and get hung up on what other people might say about the company, its size, the kind of business they are in and literally hundreds of other things that distract them from really investigating the company.

What this simply means is that, if you're a candidate, you need to be aware of the things in your background or experience that may distract a potential employer from interviewing you or realizing all of your abilities and potential once they do interview you. There may even be some positive issues that will distract a potential employer from your negative ones.

Just be aware that inattentional blindness is a reality and it has a phenomenal impact on your job search.

96. DON'T BE AFRAID OF PARANOIA.

There's nothing like a good dose of daily paranoia to get you going. Don't let anybody kid you, every one of us, even the most experienced and successful, wakes up every day with a bit of paranoia, wondering, "Can I do it again today?...Am I really that good?"

Those of us who have learned to live with paranoia find it to be a tremendously healthy emotion if it's used in the right way. There is unhealthy paranoia and healthy paranoia. We often go berserk with unhealthy paranoia when we should've been dealing with it in a healthy way, making it healthy paranoia a long time earlier. In fact, in the business situation, no matter what level you are, if you don't experience some paranoia you probably aren't doing your job. And if someone tries to tell me that they have no paranoia—even the slightest bit—that's the time I remind them that they should be afraid as hell, because they're probably at one of the biggest risk moments of their life and they don't even know it. This feeling of invincibility is the first step towards self-destruction.

Unhealthy paranoia is the kind of fear that most people get. They're afraid of everything. They're afraid of the economy. They're afraid of their company's ability to survive the difficult times. They are afraid if things are too bad, they'll go broke. They're afraid that if things are too good, everybody and their company will get apathetic and expect success. They are afraid to enjoy success because they know it, too, will end. They spend a few hours of their day commiserating with other paranoid people looking for things to be paranoid about. They begin many sentences with, "I'm afraid..." They usually follow that with the probability of how things won't work. No matter how successful they become they are still "afraid." Even when they should be on top of the world, enjoying success, they remind themselves and everyone else how afraid they are. They are no fun at all, even with millions of dollars and everything money can buy. Unfortunately, they have no courage. Most often they implode and "fail" internally despite seemingly external success. They most often die with their money but no one cares.

Healthy paranoia, on the other hand, excites. It puts us on edge. But it's a healthy fear. What separates healthy paranoia from unhealthy paranoia Is that healthy paranoia leads us to take massive action. When we lay out a massive action plan and then follow it, we can usually work our way out of our most difficult fears. These people with healthy paranoia begin every day knowing that anything can happen and they need to be ready for it.

These people with healthy paranoia look back on all of the setbacks they've had, from going broke, to losing their job, to losing their businesses, to losing loved ones prematurely to death, to experiencing just about every human difficulty you can imagine, and somehow they learn from these experiences. They appreciate the words of Frederich Nietzsche, that "what doesn't kill me, makes me stronger." This awareness gives them courage. Even though they have fear in the pit of their stomach, they know that since they've conquered it before, they can conquer it again. These are joyous, grateful people even in the gravest of situations, even with fear in their gut.

So, if you're one of those people who operates with unhealthy paranoia, try to change the way you see and experience things.

Focus on the good things paranoia has helped you to attain. Try to see how that fear in the pit of your stomach can also motivate you. Hang around, even go to work for, someone with healthy paranoia and simply ask them how they do it. Ask them what kind of "self-talk" they do.

Don't be afraid of healthy paranoia...Make it your friend and motivator.

97. DEALING WITH ILLEGAL QUESTIONS.

With the majority of companies in this country having fewer than 100 people, it probably won't surprise you that some hiring authorities just don't have any idea about what is legal and what isn't. Some will simply ask inappropriate questions, thinking that they're trying to help both you and them. I repeat: Most hiring authorities in the United States just aren't very professional. They might be good at what they do, but they're lousy when it comes to interviewing and hiring people.

Interviewers who ask illegal and inappropriate questions usually do so out of ignorance. However, some people's egos cause them to ignore the law and ask whatever they damn well please. There are hundreds of illegal interview questions. You can Google "illegal interview questions" and read them.

I happen to disagree with the experts who will tell you flat-out that, in an interview, you don't have to answer certain questions, especially ones that are illegal. I'm going to tell you to do what you think is best. I'll be the first one to tell you that illegal and inappropriate questions are completely out of line. However, if you really need the job, the legality and inappropriateness of any question is probably way down on your list of priorities. Getting a decent offer is more important.

Even if you think that the hiring or interviewing authority is aware that what he or she is asking is illegal, it may *not* be a good idea to say, "That is an illegal question and I don't have answer it," or "That is an illegal question and I won't answer it." This kind of answer will challenge the hiring authority and will probably eliminate you as a candidate.

You may want to consider answering the question, depending on the context in which it is asked. If you feel like someone is asking your age, or if you were married, because the person will probably use that information to eliminate you from consideration, then you might say something in a startled, surprised but very *kind* manner like, "Oh, goodness, I didn't know you could ask that question, but . . ." Then answer the question in a way that you think is appropriate.

You might also answer the question with a question, such as, "How does the answer to that question have an impact on my performance of the job or my ability to get it?" This is a very nice way of saying, "That's an illegal question. It has nothing to do with my ability to do the job, so I'm not going answer it." If you feel that the question is being asked out of genuine interest and in sincere empathy—as in a casual conversation after a formal interview—feel free to answer it in any manner that you wish.

Again, follow your instincts and answer these questions in whatever way you are comfortable doing. I don't think it's good to get defensive or stern about the fact that these are illegal questions. Depending on how badly you need a job, you may have to overlook some inappropriate questions, but *you need a job*. Don't let it get in the way. If you think it is appropriate to set someone straight about the illegal questions, feel free to do so. Just don't get your nose out of joint over it. If the questions insult you, don't go to work there.

98. CHANGING CAREERS.

At least four or five times a week, our organization encounters well-educated, well-trained, well-experienced professionals who want to change their careers. Their attitude is that since they have been even reasonably successful in one endeavor, they can automatically be successful in another. They look around and see people in other professions and have a tendency to think that, for one reason or another, it would be a better place for them. So, they want to change careers.

In a boom cycle, when there are fewer people and more jobs, experienced people are hard to come by. Since companies have a difficult time finding experienced people in what they specifically do, they are willing to take as close to like-kind experience as they can get and train those people. That is why some people at different times appear to have an easier time changing careers than others. The opportunity to change careers was easier in the boom economy because hiring organizations did not have much choice. They had to hire people who didn't have any experience in what they did and train them. They could afford to hire people who weren't immediately productive, train them, and not be concerned about their immediate contribution.

In a more difficult economy, however, there are lots of very qualified people available on the market and companies are watching their bottom-line profits more carefully. When earnings are harder to come by, the whole concept changes. Hiring organizations need to find people with as much experience in what they do as they can get because those people need to be contributing almost immediately to the bottom line. Companies don't think they can afford to wait around for someone to catch on to what they do. Everyone must be able to pull his or her own weight immediately. This, coupled with the fact that there are many more experienced people available in the marketplace, allows a company to be very selective in its hiring and pretty much find exactly the kind of experience that would be best.

What this means to you is that just because you think you would like to change careers doesn't mean that it is going to be feasible to do it. On top of all of this, you have to take into account the value you bring to a hiring organization when you have no track record in what they do. Why is an organization going to pay you the kind of money that you've been making doing one thing, or in one profession, to perform in a position or function that you have either absolutely no, or very little, experience doing?

Since 1973, I've been interviewing thousands of candidates who have wanted to change their careers. For one reason or another, they want to get out of what they're doing and into something else. About 98% of the time, they still need to earn the same kind of money as they have been earning in their present field. Neat trick.

I hear things like, "My neighbor is the president [or comptroller, vice president, or whatever] of a big company. He is a schmuck. He's a lousy husband and father, and everybody knows he is an idiot. I know I can do a better job than he can. So I want a job like that." Or, I hear things like, "Well, you know, the green movement is really catching on and I've read there's a lot of money in it. I've been really successful in everything I've done, so find me a job in something that has potential in green technology."

Most of the books on career change aren't realistic. They give examples that are the exceptions to the rule rather than the common situation. If you are going to try to shift into any career that's even reasonably competitive, it's going to be an uphill battle. Michael Jordan was a great athlete—the best basketball player in the world—but when he tried to play baseball, he was not as successful. In spite of his hard work and natural athletic ability, he was competing with guys who were solid baseball players. They may not have been as good an athlete as he was, but they were better baseball players. So, when the big leagues were looking for documentable baseball skills, Michael Jordan wasn't at the top of the list. He went back to basketball.

What most of the career change "experts" neglect to mention is that the further away you get from your documented skills or demonstrated knowledge, the harder it is to get hired. Unless you're willing to either start over at the bottom or take a drastic cut in pay—and even then it is difficult—changing careers is a near impossibility. Why do you suppose lots of career-changing folks start their own businesses? Because they have a hard time getting a job with someone else!

Once in a while a sector of business emerges for which there is very little "like-kind" experience among job seekers. Back in the mid-'90s, when computer technology was being developed for business, there were few salespeople who had experience in the profession of selling hardware and software solutions. So companies recruited good salespeople from payroll services, real estate, and just about any other field involving sales and hired them. We're now, however, in our third or fourth iteration of technology. Many of these software and hardware firms have contracted, merged, or gone away. Advanced technology has made many of these solutions a commodity. And as the technology has advanced, the opportunity to make a lot of money in selling software or hardware has diminished.

We still get candidates who claim that, since they're very good at selling insurance, or real estate, or whatever, they want to change careers and sell software because it is more lucrative.

They say, with a straight face, "I saw a job you advertised where the earnings are $250,000 per year. I need to make that kind of money, so get me the interview." They have no idea that they're competing with experienced salespeople who got into the software and hardware business years ago. Why would a company hire an unproven person when people with documentable skills and successes are available?

Those people who want to change careers say things like, "But I know I can do it." Okay, maybe you can, but it is going to be rare for a company to take a chance on you when they can hire a person with direct experience. And when unemployment is high and the market is flooded with all kinds of people having all kinds of experience, getting hired to do something you have no documented skills in and still make reasonable earnings is going to be even harder.

Most people who successfully change careers either go into a profession not saturated at the time, like teaching or healthcare, or they open their own business and run the risks themselves. But, similarly, most career-change books don't tell people how hard it is to run a business. A lot of new businesses fail because the people who start them have absolutely no idea how to run a business.

What to do? If you are considering changing careers, first get tested to see if you have the aptitude to do what you have in mind. For instance, if you want a career in playing music, but find out you are tone-deaf, you may want to reconsider. We all know people who thought they were good at a particular hobby, but once they tried to turn that hobby into a business, they failed. So, for a first step, assess your skills and aptitudes to see where your strengths are. And don't rely on cheap online programs to do this assessment. The Johnson O'Connor

Foundation, a nonprofit organization, does an excellent job of giving people an assessment of their aptitudes.

Be prepared to start at the bottom, no matter what you decide to do. Even if you can get someone to hire you in a business you know absolutely nothing about, you're still going to have to prove yourself. The probability of you being hired in a business you know nothing about, by someone who doesn't know you, at a decent salary, isn't very likely.

You might want to consider a career adjustment rather than a career change. If you can, try to find a profession or job that somehow relates to the kind of thing you've been doing, so that you can bring something to the party. This, at least, gives you some advantage.

Let me make it emphatically clear that changing careers is possible. But most people don't take into account everything that it entails. In the previous example, if a person were to start all over at the ground floor of a profession and work his or her way up, it is feasible. This usually means a drastic cut in earnings. Why would a company, on average, pay top dollar to a person whose experience and background doesn't fit exactly what they want done? If a person has a father-in-law, brother-in-law, relative, or very close friend who is willing to pay what he or she has been making to do a job that he or she really doesn't know how to do, or has no track record in, it might work.

So, to change careers you're most likely going to have to make it a good business deal for a prospective employer — worth the risk involved in taking on someone without proven experience. You'll have to say something along the line of, "Look, I've been a successful accountant for the past 15 years, but I want be a real estate appraiser. I'm working on certifications. I'm willing to go to work for half of what you would normally pay an appraiser.

I am willing to start out at the bottom and work my way up. I am a good employee. I will make the risk worthwhile for you."

There is always the option of owning your own business. There are tremendous amounts of entrepreneurial and franchise opportunities available in U.S. business. (Did you know that one of the industries that has created more millionaires from scratch in the United States is the dry-cleaning business? It certainly isn't exotic and it has its problems, but it can be extremely lucrative.) Owning one's own business, especially a small business, in the United States is a lot more difficult than most people think.

But, everything has its price and there are plenty of millionaires who got into the business that made them money because they had no other choice. It appears that success in owning your own business, in either a standalone or franchise opportunity, boils down to the same things that any other successful business does—no matter what the size, find a system that works and stick to it.

If you have already changed careers and are looking to get back into a profession in which you had previous experience before your most recent career change, you are experiencing the same difficulty that those people who want to change careers are experiencing.

A few years ago, I had a candidate who, after spending 15 years selling software, bought a chain of retail dry-cleaning stores. He was very successful and had the chance to sell the stores at a sizable profit. He really didn't like all the business problems he encountered in the dry-cleaning business, so he wanted to get back into selling software. He had a hard time even getting interviews, let alone job offers.

First, he didn't have any recent contacts or recent track record in the software business and second, all of the other candidates he was competing with did. Although he had a tremendous track record up until he went into the dry-cleaning business, there were too many other candidates out there, especially in this market, ones who weren't as great a risk. Prospective employers would say things like, "Well, Tony, if he really wanted to sell software, why did he get out of it?" Or, "Well, Tony, we can't run the risk of hiring this guy even if his track record was good, because, after a year or so, he may decide to do something else entrepreneurial. And the last thing we need is for someone to get into the job for a year or so and then leave."

The success that a person might have in returning to a profession or career that was interrupted by a completely different profession or career will depend on timing. If the economy is in a boom cycle and the ratio of candidates to job opportunities is low, then the hiring organization has to take the best candidate who is available, even if his or her experience might be two or three years old. But, if the economy is like it has been in recent years—where the ratio of qualified candidates to job opportunities is high—competition is very keen, so the hiring organization can take fewer risks.

How can you overcome the fact that you're changing or have changed careers? Knock on lots of doors until you find someone who will accept the risk!

99. RESIGN THE RIGHT WAY...GRACEFULLY.

If you were unemployed and have recently found a job, resigning is not a crucial issue to you. However, if you are currently employed, and especially if you have been for a fairly long period of time (five years or more by today's standards), leaving your job may be harder than you think. You should be prepared for your own trepidation. Even if your resignation ought to be an easy thing to do, it is still emotionally charged, and *doing it the right way* makes a really big difference.

Whether you think resigning is going to be emotionally easy on both you and your employer, or not, you need to be prepared to do it the right way so that you don't burn any bridges on the way out.

I've had candidates resign by email. I've known people to just not show up for their job and, three or four days later, call their supervisor to tell the person that they are resigning. In other cases, they simply did not show but never called; after a number of days, it was just assumed that they had left the company. None of these is the right way to do things.

People will often resort to this type of final exit simply because they are nervous, scared, and just don't want to face up to the task of gracefully resigning. Most people mentally and emotionally leave the job a long time before they actually physically leave. They are so mentally and emotionally spent and so sick of the whole thing that they just want to leave as fast as possible.

Where this sort of thing comes back to haunt them is in a reference check. It is common for a previous manager, even though he or she knows better, to tell someone who is checking a reference in a situation like this to say something along the lines of, "Well, when he or she left here, it was a real mess." A poor reference is implied simply by communicating a veiled aura of negativity surrounding the previous employee's departure from a company.

There are some people who will have a more difficult time than others in resigning. If you fall into any of the following categories that I'm going to mention, be prepared for the process to be a little more difficult than you thought. The kinds of people who have the most difficult time in resigning are:

- *First-time job changers.* You feel guilty about leaving the company that gave you your first chance.
- *Longtime employees.* You feel like you have grown up with the company; it's hard to say goodbye.
- *Those who hint about leaving all the time.* You have repeatedly threatened to leave before and now you really are!
- *Single-reason leavers.* You may be reluctant to tell the single reason for you wanting to leave or you may be afraid your reason sounds insignificant to others, although it is important to you.
- *Multifaceted/multitask person.* You're the kind of person who has significant influence in the company; you feel like you are letting everybody down by leaving.
- *Family member.* You are either immediately or closely related to the people who own or manage the company.

Always resign with a written letter. Be resolute and firm in your commitment to resign. You cannot afford a weak or ambivalent attitude. Here's a sample resignation letter:

Date_____

Dear [direct supervisor's name]:

My resignation from the position of [current title] is effective as of today.

I really appreciate and will always remember my experience in working with you and [your company]. Thank you for what you've taught me over the [a period of time] and for the many contributions that you have made to my personal

*and professional development. I truly hope that we can stay
in touch from time to time in the years ahead.*

*I will always have positive memories about the profession-
alism at [your company].*

*The status of my work is up-to-date and I will turn it over to
whomever you designate.*

Sincerely,
[Your name]

That's it! Do not make the letter more complicated than
this. Do not teach, preach, cajole, or elaborate as to why you're
leaving. Many people want to set 'em straight, tell them where
they went wrong, tell them where they can get off, explain to
them why they have a stupid company, list what they ought to
do to fix the company, and so forth. You're wasting your breath.
You are leaving and they don't care what you think.

Resign with a face-to-face meeting. Be relaxed and easy.
Don't be nervous. Take a deep breath. Play a movie in your
mind that it's going to go very smoothly. Practice the scenario
in a role-play with your coach. You want to be aggressive and
prepared. Do not make an appointment to resign. Simply go
to your supervisor during a regular, workday moment and say,
"May I speak with you a moment?"

You should only resign to one person. Do not convene
a group or committee. Doing so creates a one-against-many
situation and the emotional odds are against you. Resign with
your direct supervisor. Try to do it in person, unless your
supervisor is in a distant city and you must do it by phone.

If you have to resign from a distance, have a telephone
conversation before you either send or email the letter. If you

think that there is going to be a negative emotional response to your leaving, you want to communicate person-to-person. Begin by thanking your boss for all the opportunities that he or she and the company have given you. Even if you hate the person, the job, and the company, it is hard for a person to have an acrimonious conversation when you are thanking him or her.

Be sure to include in your opening statement that you have already accepted another position and that you are going to be leaving the company. Say something like this:

> *Mr. or Ms._____, I have accepted another employment opportunity and I want to give notice today. I'd like to thank you for making a real contribution to my career development. I would like to do everything possible during the next [time frame] to make my transition out of your department and the company a smooth one. What is the easiest way for us to make this transition?*

If the boss tries to engage you in conversation about the new job, or the offer, or says, "How could you do this to me or us?" or even hints at a counteroffer, preempt his or her comments by saying:

> *[Name], I think you know I really respect our relationship a lot and I know that this comes as a surprise to you. However, I would really appreciate it if you would not try to make the process of my resignation any more difficult than it has to be. [pause] I have accepted another opportunity, and I appreciate all that you've done but I am resolute about leaving. I have made my decision. I ask for your understanding. Now, what is the easiest way to make this transition?*

You might also add:

I have taken the liberty of writing up all of the projects I am working on and their current status. If you could take a moment with me to review them in the next day or so, I'd be happy to do anything I can to complete them or hand them over during the next [time frame].

Do not go into resigning by stating that you are thinking about taking another position, or that you are thinking about changing jobs, or anything that is wishy-washy and spineless. You must go in with the decisive, factual "I have taken another job" statement. This has to be an absolute fact, not a whim.

Be prepared to preempt a counteroffer. Even entertaining the idea of a counteroffer is suicide. If you go on and on about how difficult a decision it was or how hard you thought about it, or how you talked it over with your spouse, you not only compromise your position, but you appear weak and pitiful.

Offer two weeks' notice. Even if you know that the company will want you to leave immediately, you still want to be courteous and offer two weeks. *Do not offer more than two weeks!* It is not good for you or your company. You have mentally and emotionally left a long time ago. You're gone—so physically leave as soon as you can.

It is best not to gloat about your new job or your new company. It isn't good to brag about the opportunity for which you are leaving. There is a tendency to be proud of your new job and run off at the mouth about the new opportunity, as though to say, "Wow, look at me, guess what I've got!" Simply remember that you are resigning, not competing. Stay away from lecturing or trying to instruct the company on how they ought to change things in the future so people like you wouldn't leave. It will only insult them.

It is advisable not to discuss your new job, your new company, or all the reasons that you are leaving with any of your peers, subordinates, or anyone else in the company. Your leaving should not be a topic of conversation with you or with anyone else. Even if your parting is amiable, once you quit, the relationship with everyone is strained. Make it simple and easy for everybody.

100. STARTING A NEW JOB.

Most people think that once they have started a new job, their job search is over. I am continually amazed at the strange things that can take place even after a person has started a new job.

The first bit of advice is for you to expect that the job is going to be quite a bit different from what you thought it was going to be when you were going through the interviewing process. Things are never the way they appear on the outside looking in.

The second suggestion is to spend the first few weeks or even months simply observing what goes on in the company. The higher the position that you may have, the more you want to quietly observe how the company is run. You really want to get a good idea of what is going on in the company before you start actively showing people what you can do for them.

The best way to find out what really goes on in an organization is to talk to the most senior-level administrative personnel (we used to call them secretaries). These people know more about what is going on in the inner workings of the organization than anybody else. Now, these people may not be the decision makers in an organization, but they still know more of what is going on in a company than all the managers combined.

Get to know your supervisor's personality and style. Do this with all the people with whom you might interface. Remember that you are the new kid on the block and that you don't know the character or personality of the people, or the part, of the organization that you are working with.

Don't hesitate to ask lots and lots of questions regarding procedures and protocols. Nobody expects you to be intuitive about anything. It may not hurt to take notes about what you learn, especially regarding the unofficial procedures. A friend of mine who has been a "work" psychologist for 40 years, Frank Lawlis, tells the story that the best advice he got about starting a new job was to "be quiet and walk around for about six months before you start trying to sound off." Whatever you do, don't offer your opinions about issues or topics outside of business, like politics or religion.

Take lots of notes when you go into meetings and try to write down who said what. Once you get to know these people and know who stands where on certain things, it's good to take notes about who they are. Also, it helps to write their names down a number of times so you can remember them.

Recognize and avoid the negative people who exist within every organization. They can range from the people who always see the glass half-empty to the people who are downright negative, gossipy, and in some cases, slanderous. Avoid them like the plague.

The most important thing you can do as a professional when beginning a new job is to be quiet and try not to draw attention to yourself until you really learn about the company and the personalities of the people from the inside. Too often, newly hired professionals try to make an immediate impact to show how good they are by drawing attention to themselves in a number of ways before they really know the so-called lay of the land.

No matter how good you might be, no matter how smart you are, no matter how much you might be able to contribute to the organization, you will have much more impact and be received with much more respect if you learn as much as you can about the organization and its personalities before you start having significant input. There is going to be plenty of time to prove yourself.

101. HOW TO LOVE YOUR JOB.

I discovered a few simple, not necessarily easy, but simple principles that people who love their job practice:

They assess and know their aptitudes.

Most of us fall into what we have an aptitude for quite by accident. We try enough things and then fall into a job or career that might take advantage of our natural abilities, but aptitude testing may quickly reveal most of our strengths and weaknesses. When aptitudes are honed and well-developed, we end up calling them gifts. But those polished gifts didn't start out that way. They were raw to begin with.

They expect to begin as a total novice and then work really, really, really hard...and discover flow and the zone.

Working really hard means accepting ignorance, then breaking down the basic functions of the job and then doing them over and over until they are mastered. This means an investment of a phenomenal amount of time and effort even when they are exhausted and want to quit.

They seek the intrinsic value in what they do.

They look for their own personal, internal growth and satisfaction as much as they do in perfecting what they do. They practice what they do for the sheer fun and joy of doing it and because it makes them feel good as they are growing; it takes on a life of its own.

They really love and are passionate about what they do.

Next to their relationship with God and their family, they enjoy what they do more than anything else. They often enjoy it more than they want to eat or sleep. They are so passionate and enthusiastic about it, what they do becomes a part of them and they become a part of what they do. They personally identify with their work and it brings them joy and happiness. They often have to force themselves to step away and refresh.

They do it for a purpose or vision greater than they are.

The purpose of doing what they do transcends making a living. They see the purpose of what they do in the light of its impact on others, even all of mankind. It takes on a spiritual dimension that's greater than the activity. This greater purpose transforms their work and their job into a calling. It is a personal mission to affect the greater world with their work.

They have a healthy balance of paranoia, courage, and grit.

Everyone who loves their career and their job lives with a permanent amount of paranoia. No matter how accomplished they become they always hear a little voice inside of them asking themselves, "Are you really that good? Can I do it again today?"

Courage in this metaphor is the faith and the confidence that I can and will run. Courage gives me the confidence to practice running, which gives me more courage to run harder and faster. Courage counterbalances the paranoid and keeps paranoia from simply freezing me from inactivity.

Grit is the experience in our metaphor of running "until I am totally exhausted, but have the perseverance and passion to get up and keep running." The tension between paranoia and courage leads to creativity.

They have great clarity and simplicity in explaining what they do.

Their clarity is astounding. They explain what they do in its simplest format. This doesn't mean that what they do is easy! Just because they can explain it simply doesn't mean that it is easy. Bench-pressing 500 pounds is simple but it's not easy. In fact, it's hard...very hard.

They develop a system, a process of doing business and personal rituals and routine for life.

Most of the people who love and develop their career live routine lives with lots of rituals. They develop specific patterns for living that allow their cognitive and emotional efforts to focus on their work. They don't have to expend a lot of emotional or mental energy in deciding which white shirt to wear or which black pair of socks to choose or what time to meditate every day. Rituals and routines alleviate the conscious energy needed to make small inconsequential decisions. Those routine decisions, added together, take a tremendous amount of mental and emotional effort. Rituals and routines conserve mental and emotional energy so it can be used for the creative aspects of work.

Finding mentors and being a constant student, then becoming a mentor.

Some of us are fortunate enough to simply fall into finding good teachers.

Hopefully, the mentors we find are good practitioners and good leaders, but bad leaders can often be great practitioners. We may be able to learn a practice or skill from someone who might be a jerk. The physician who has the habit of smoking might be a great practitioner of medicine, but a lousy mentor of what to do. We can learn from skilled practitioners who might be lousy human beings. We can learn from bad managers. Maybe we learn what not to do or how not to be from these people.

Humility and gratitude.

The kind of people we're speaking of have a tremendous amount of humility. Their accomplishments never seem to go to their head. In fact, most often they don't think their accomplishments or successes are that big a deal. They don't compare themselves to other people, they compare themselves to their own perception of their potential. Since they are always striving to be better they gracefully accept what they have accomplished. They have a healthy ego but not a big ego.

We reframe stories of our past...and write stories of our future.

When I was 10 years old I wrote a story of myself being Superman. When I learned I couldn't fly I reframed this story that at least I could become the strongest man on earth. When I imagined a story of myself becoming a doctor when I went to college, I reframed my story when I had to drop out of freshman chemistry right before I failed it. When I imagined the story of getting a PhD in higher education and becoming president of a college in 1973, my beautiful wife Chris reframed that story when I couldn't find a job by explaining to me that she was pregnant with our first child, I had no job, and we'd better get to Texas and go to work.

Final thought: What you become in the process of getting what you want is more important than what you get.

This is the last and probably the most important rule of a job search. It is an important rule for just about every endeavor we may take on. How we grow spiritually and emotionally in any kind of important "life" endeavor is more important and more permanent than anything we acquire, including a job. Jobs and careers can come and go, but how we grow on the inside, how we grow personally is forever.

No matter how difficult, challenging, or successful a job search might be, we all need to analyze how it affects our emotions, heart, and soul. We need to be constantly asking ourselves, "Am I becoming a better person in the process of getting what I want?"

I remind people all the time that nearly everything we do materialistically affects our heart, soul, and character. Sometimes we are well aware of it and sometimes we forget how what we're doing is going to affect our spiritual growth.

Our newspapers are full of stories daily of people who seem to "have it all" and because they didn't pay attention to feeding their heart and their soul, they implode. They grew externally but didn't pay attention to growing internally. When the external far outweighs the internal the façade of success can't be supported. The emotions, heart, and soul can't support the weight of the success. It is often tragic that these people not only destroy themselves but also others along with them.

So pay attention to how you are growing on the inside as well as how you were growing on the outside. Is your job search helping you grow as a person...your heart, your mind, your soul, your character? What we become in the process of getting what we want is more permanent and everlasting than what we acquire. Our possessions, our jobs, our career can all come and go. None of them are ends in themselves. They are only means by which we grow. In the words of Aleksandr Solzhenitsyn: "The purpose of this life is not prosperity as we know it, but rather the maturing of the human soul."

To view my TED Talk "The Principles of People Who Love Their Job and Their Career," please visit youtube.com/watch?v=iuxoNtqfNEM.

ABOUT THE AUTHOR

Tony Beshara is the owner and president of Babich & Associates, established in 1952, which is the oldest placement and recruitment service in Texas. It is one of the top contingency placement firms in the DFW area as recognized by the *Dallas-Ft. Worth Business Journal*.

Tony is in the trenches daily. A professional recruiter since 1973, Tony has personally found more than 11,000 jobs for individuals, has personally interviewed more than 26,000 people on all professional levels, and has worked with more than 23,000 hiring authorities. Babich & Associates has helped more than 100,000 people find jobs using Tony's proven process. Tony Beshara is one of the most successful placement and recruitment professionals in the United States.

Tony received his Ph.D. in Higher Education from St. Louis University. He is a published author of several titles, including:

- *The Job Search Solution: The Ultimate System for Finding a Great Job NOW!* The second edition of this bestselling book published January 2012.

- *Acing The Interview*, another bestseller, answers almost any question regarding interviewing in today's erratic job market.
- *Powerful Phrases for Successful Interviews*, published February 2014, offers 400 ideal phases for every interviewing situation.
- *100,000 Successful Hires, The Art, Science and Luck of Successful Hiring*, co-authored with Rich Lavinski, covers the "other side" of the desk—advice for the hiring authority. It, too, is a bestseller.

Tony Beshara is a frequent guest on the *Dr. Phil* show, offering Dr. Phil's guests advice on the job search process, as well as on *The Willis Report* televised on Fox Business. He has created a 45-hour online program about how to find a job, found at www.TheJobSearchSolution.com. Tony hosts a daily radio show, "The Job Search Solution" on KVCE, 1160 AM, Monday through Friday from 8 to 8:30 pm. Tony and his beautiful wife of forty-seven years have four sons.